W9-ANK-501

This is a timely and important book for Christian men (and the women who know them). Bill intersperses a biblical perspective of leadership—in the workplace, the family, the church, and the community—with practical examples from real life to demonstrate how to put those principles into action. In a day when some are questioning the "feminization of the Church," this book shows men how to be "real men" and godly leaders.

Chuck Colson, Founder, Prison Fellowship

Are you looking for satisfaction and significance? Or, have you ever desired to make a name, maybe even an eternal name, in a nameless world? Have you longed to be a leader in your community, your workplace, or your church? Have you been wondering what it would take to be a better man, a better husband, and a better father? Is your heart calling out to you to become a man, a real man? Then my dear friend, Bill Peel, has written the guidebook and handbook for which you've been searching. Marinate your soul in this book's teachings and principles. Chew and digest it slowly and carefully. Apply it, one principle and one day at a time, and watch with amazement the transformation your Creator will accomplish in and through you.

Walt Larimore, MD, Coauthor, *His Brain, Her Brain: How Divinely Designed Differences Can Strengthen Your Marriage*

Inspiring! Practical! Comprehensive! I have read a boatload of leadership books but this is by far the best. It's helped me to be a better father, husband, and leader in every sphere of my life. Every man should read it.

David Stevens, MD, Chief Executive Officer, Christian Medical & Dental Associations

Churches today are filled with what the world needs most—leaders. Rather than offering them meaningful opportunities to be involved in Kingdom work, many pastors inadvertently give men the message that there is not a role for them. The disturbing result is diminished Kingdom impact. Bill Peel gives men keen insight into the myriad of Kingdom opportunities waiting for them, not only in the church, but at home, on the job, and in their communities. If you are waiting to "get into the game" but find yourself on the sidelines, this is a must read.

Tom Wilson, President and CEO, Leadership Network

WHAT GOD DOES WHEN MEN LEAD

The Power and
Potential of
Regular Guys

BILL PEEL

Tyndale House Publishers, Inc.
Carol Stream, Illinois

Visit Tyndale's exciting Web site at www.tyndale.com

TYNDALE and Tyndale's quill logo are registered trademarks of Tyndale House Publishers, Inc.

What God Does When Men Lead: The Power and Potential of Regular Guys

Cover designed by Erik Peterson

Interior designed by Timothy R. Botts

Library of Congress Cataloging-in-Publication Data

Peel, William Carr.
  What God does when men lead : the power and potential of regular guys / Bill Peel.
     p. cm.
  Includes bibliographical references.
  ISBN-13: 978-1-4143-1549-2 (hc)
  ISBN-10: 1-4143-1549-X (hc)
  1. Christian men—Religious life. 2. Leadership—Religious aspects—Christianity. I. Title.
  BV4528.2.P44 2008
  248.8′42—dc22   2007046767

Printed in the United States of America

14   13   12   11   10   09   08
7   6   5   4   3   2   1

To
John, Joel, and James Peel,
who are discovering for themselves
what God does when men lead

CONTENTS

Acknowledgments

The voices of many teachers, mentors, and leaders echo throughout the pages of this book. If you've read C. S. Lewis, Dorothy Sayers, or George MacDonald, you'll recognize familiar thoughts. If you attend Redeemer Presbyterian Church in Manhattan or download Tim Keller's sermons, there's a place or two where you may hear his voice with a Texas accent.

I am grateful to John Van Deist and Jan Long Harris for providing the encouragement and opportunity to capture in words what I've learned (mostly the hard way) about living as a man attempting to follow Jesus. Sincere thanks also go to my editor, Kim Miller, who patiently translated my Texican into proper English, as well as Nancy Clausen, Sarah Atkinson, Sharon Leavitt, Yolanda Sidney, Maggie Rowe, Bonne Steffen, and the entire Tyndale team.

As the father of three sons, biblical manhood was never an academic exercise or just about me. John, Joel, and James Peel needed me to get this as right as I could. Now it's their job to discover what God does when men lead. When John and Joel became husbands and leaders of their own homes last year, I was reminded again of God's wonderful wisdom in making mankind both male and female. I love watching Genevieve and Christin love my boys and help them become the men God created them to be.

According to George MacDonald, the chief duty of a husband and wife is to help each other do the will of God. After thirty-six years of marriage, Kathy still takes that responsibility seriously. She has given me the opportunity to learn to be a man and encourages me to accept nothing less than becoming the man God intended me to be. I am forever grateful for this woman God sent into my life.

I also want to thank Chuck Hamilton, Steve Blankenship, Pretlow Riddick, and Tracy Taylor, who work together with me to help bring Kingdom reality to the workplace in Dallas.

Where Have All the Leaders Gone?

A lot of guys I know are La-Z-Boy leaders. From our recliner-and-command post, armed with our remote, we can see precisely what the president and the coach of our favorite NFL team are doing wrong. "Where are the Abraham Lincolns ... the John Kennedys ... and the Tom Landrys when we need them?" we rant. "We need some guys with vision and integrity to get things back on track!"

Having said our piece, we switch channels and learn that the stock market—and thus our retirement fund—has taken a hit, which brings out our inner Warren Buffet. "If those sorry CEOs would focus on business instead of lining their pockets, we'd all be in better shape," we blurt out between generous bites of ice cream. "Where'd they find these so-called leaders anyway—under a rock? They're all snakes! Are there any real leaders left in the world?"

Those are fair questions that deserve some thought because the problem is obviously not a shortage of leadership candidates. Universities graduate thousands, groomed for greatness, every year. There's an overabundance of organizational climbers, young and old, ready to do whatever it takes to grasp that next rung on the leadership ladder.

If you are concerned about the quality of leadership in our country, you're not alone. Two-thirds of Americans believe we are experiencing a leadership crisis. Three-quarters of us worry about what will become of our nation if we don't find better leaders soon.[1]

Eight out of ten Americans believe that corporate executives are less concerned with running their companies than they are with lining their own pockets.[2] You don't need an accounting degree to see that the numbers don't add up when you compare the growth of CEO compensation with the growth rate of your investments.

The problem is not a shortage of leaders but of *worthy* leaders—men who want to serve rather than be served. Men who are not driven by making a name for themselves, but who want to help others succeed. Men who are willing to sacrifice personal interests for the interests of others. Men who ask where they can make the most significant contribution rather than where they can make the most money.

There is a second element to the problem as well. Although most men desire roles of greater leadership at work, many become noticeably passive when it comes to spiritual, cultural, and familial issues—causing serious and far-reaching harm. Yet male passivity is not a new problem. The Bible recounts the stories of many men—Moses, Abraham, Eli, David, Peter, and others—who chose passivity when they needed to take action. Dr. Larry Crabb pinpoints the core problem.

> Since Adam, every man has had a natural inclination to remain silent when he should speak. A man is most comfortable in situations in which he knows exactly what to do. When things get confusing and scary, his insides tighten and he backs away. When life frustrates him with its maddening unpredictability, he feels the anger rise within him. And then, filled with terror and rage, he forgets God's truth and looks out for himself. From then on, everything goes wrong. Committed only to himself, he scrambles to make his own life work. The result is what we see every day: sexual passions out of control, uninvolved husbands and fathers, angry men who love to be in the driver's seat. And it all began when Adam refused to speak.[3]

Note to Male Readers

If you bought this book for yourself, I commend you for taking the initiative. If your wife, girlfriend, or mother gave you this book, or if a church leader decided this would be a good topic for your small group to study, you may be wondering why they selected it for you. No matter how the book came into your possession, by reading it you are taking an important step of self-leadership, which is where we all must begin to become the leaders God wants us to be.

> *The price of greatness is responsibility.*
> WINSTON CHURCHILL

I think you will discover that *What God Does When Men Lead* is different from the leadership books that occupy significant shelf space in bookstores today. For example, numerous books on leadership focus on one area, such as organizational or community leadership, but this book covers every area of a man's life. Many other books tell you how to be leaderlike—how to dress, run a meeting, and exude an aura of confidence. There are even books that coach you on how to shake hands, answer the phone, and order from a menu like a leader. You won't find those topics in this book—not that these things are necessarily bad. It's just that they don't have much to do with leadership—at least from God's point of view.

According to God, leadership is more about who you are and the choices you make. It's about believing that what He says about you is more important than what press clippings or your résumé says about you. It's about understanding that putting on the armor of God is infinitely more empowering than putting on an expensive suit and power tie. It's about what drives you—not what you drive.

It is our substance, not style, that qualifies us for leadership. And our substance—the stuff at the core of our being—is formed from the choices we make day by day, hour by hour, at the private, intimate levels of life. Who we are up close and personal is the proving ground of true leadership.

At the end of each chapter you will find a section called "Living as a Faithful Steward" with questions for personal reflection and small group discussion. I encourage you to ponder and personalize the principles that hit home with you in each chapter. Take time to write down your thoughts and make them your own. Discussing them in a group will help you even more.

Note to Female Readers

If you are a woman, I realize that this book may cause angst. Understandably, it is painful to recall hard-fought battles that opened new vistas for you. It hurts to remember the abuse many of you have endured under domineering males. And it's frustrating to consider the lost contributions of women kept "under control" by culturally imposed roles and expectations. Even now, if you are shouldering responsibilities that should be shared with men, you may be thinking, *I'm sick and tired of doing all the work while they sit around.*

Please understand that when I talk about male leadership, I don't mean it in a "men lead, women don't" sense or a zero-sum-game dominance contest. In no way do I question that women are leaders, nor do I want to deprive them of any leadership role God intends for them. To do so would be patently unbiblical and would discount the tremendous contributions of many female leaders, not to mention raise the ire of my thirty-six-year partner in marriage, who has unquestionable leadership abilities. But even more important, to stop women from exercising any God-given gift would anger the One who distributed that gift in the first place.

This book is meant to guide and encourage men to become the leaders God intends us to be, living in such a way that women (and other men, for that matter) want to follow us. I'll be first in line to confess that we men have not been careful to honor the gifts and dignity of the people we lead—especially the women in our lives.

You Are Called to Be a Leader

In various places and seasons of life, every one of us is called to lead—in our families, at the workplace, at church, and in the community—no matter how many people are following (or not following). In different ways and means, God commands us to step up and take responsibility, influence those around us for good, and transform the corner of planet earth where we live and work for His glory.[4]

The premise of this book is simple: God made men to lead—and we're not. Men are not assuming the responsible leadership roles God wants us to take. As a result, our faith remains underdeveloped, and we fail to impact our sphere of influence as God intended. However, when we do step up to the plate, take our God-given leadership assignment seriously, and lead in God's way, seriously good things can happen—in every area of our lives and the world at large.

What might God do if you embrace your leadership mandate? For starters, He could restore intimacy with your wife and repair relationships with your children. He could use you to transform your workplace. He could make you a seen or unseen force that changes your church for God's glory. He could use you to bring justice, fairness, and morality back to your community. He could cause your influence to discourage environmental abuse. He could use you to change the world.

And what might happen if you don't take the call to leadership seriously? Well, just watch the evening news and you'll get the picture.

You will find that the biblical leadership to which we men are called is not difficult or complicated. We don't need an exceptional education or a Pattonesque personality to be a leader. There are just two basic things God calls us to do: First, He calls us to take responsibility for ourselves. Second, He calls us to nurture and develop the resources and people He has entrusted to our care. These are things any man can do, and every man has been called to do. In the chapters that follow you will learn sensible, practical, and biblical ways to do this in every area of your life.

It is our choice either to sit back and passively respond to the happenings of each day or take seriously God's command to be His follower and a leader of those He has entrusted to our care.

May we choose well. A lot is at stake.

BILL PEEL

PART ONE
PERSPECTIVE

A man who becomes conscious of the responsibility he bears toward a human being who affectionately waits for him, or to an unfinished work, will never be able to throw away his life. He knows the "why" for his existence, and will be able to bear almost any "how."
VICTOR FRANKL

If your actions inspire others to dream more, learn more, do more, and become more, you are a leader.
JOHN QUINCY ADAMS

Whoever wants to become great among you must be your servant, and whoever wants to be first must be slave of all. For even the Son of Man did not come to be served, but to serve, and to give his life as a ransom for many.
MARK 10:43-45

CHAPTER 1

Wanted: A New Kind of Leader

The first responsibility of a leader is to define reality. The last is to say thank you. In between, the leader is a servant and a debtor.   MAX DE PREE

Do you think of yourself as a leader? If an image of George Patton or Jack Welch pops into your mind when you hear the word *leader*, you—like most other guys—would have to say no. But at some place, every man is a leader. That includes you. Whether you think of yourself as a leader or not, if you want to please God, it is crucial for you to understand what God wants of leaders. Sadly, there is a lot of confusion about leadership.

The last half of the twentieth century marked a shift in the way people think about leadership. Prior to the 1980s, we talked about managers and managing—people who were trained and could get things done. Leadership was considered more of a personality trait than a professional skill. But in the 1980s, the idea of leadership—the ability to cast a vision for the future, to transform what *is* into what *could be*—captured our imaginations. Americans have always liked the idea of a White Knight who could ride in and deliver us from our problems. Ronald Reagan delivered us from the Evil Empire. Lee Iacocca delivered Chrysler, its shareholders, and thousands of workers from economic disaster. FedEx founder Fred Smith delivered us from waiting days for mail and late packages. Rudy Giuliani saved New York City from a soaring crime rate. We like people who give us hope. And better still, we like people who can provide what we hope for.

As more and more Americans found their investment portfolios growing in the 1980s and 90s, we inflated the value of those individuals who had the ability (or so we thought) to turn companies around and increase the return on our investments. We elevated them, along with their compensation packages, to the level of superstars. To be sure, some leaders have earned their status, performing sacrificially and with excellence to the benefit of others. Some leaders have turned around crumbling companies and saved the jobs of thousands. Others have risked their last dime and endured ridicule to build multibillion-dollar companies that make our lives better in many ways. In no way am I suggesting that these individuals deserve blame or shame.

What I am suggesting is that when we look to a single person in power to change a company, government, community, church, or even a family, we do ourselves—and those individuals—a great disservice. When we place our complete trust in those at the top to "fix things," we fall into the trap of expecting someone else to fix our lives. As a result, we become frustrated and blame others when life doesn't turn out as we expected. Ken Lay wasn't the only person responsible for Enron's shady dealings and demise. Michael Brown was not solely to blame for FEMA's sluggish response to the Katrina disaster.

When we credit one person for an outcome that required the work of many people, we also set up that person for personal defeat. The temptation to believe that an organization's success was his doing alone has ruined many a man. "[We have] a wrongheaded notion of what exactly a leader is. This misguided notion of leadership often results in the wrong people attaining critical leadership roles. Search committees and voters alike fall into the trap of choosing leaders for their style rather than their substance, for their image instead of their integrity. Given this way of doing business, why should we be surprised when our leaders come up short?" writes business journalist Bill George.[1]

Media outlets can be counted on to showcase the failures of today's leaders, giving special attention to those leaders who do not hold their particular "unbiased" bias. Yet cable TV and Internet blogs were not the first to document the problems of those at the top. The Bible also records the shortfalls and outright failures of many leaders, providing powerful lessons we can apply today. Take Moses, a guy I consider to be recorded history's first world-class leader.

If ever a leader qualified for pedestal placement, it was Moses. Miraculously saved from drowning, he was raised as the darling child of Egyptian aristocracy. Moses probably knew from a young age that he was a man of destiny and purpose. But when his purpose to deliver his fellow Jews from cruel bondage became clear, he made the mistake of trusting in his own power and prowess to bring about his destiny. Without stopping to consider God's timing, Moses murdered an Egyptian middle-manager, then tried to cover up his crime by burying the victim in the sand—all in pursuit of his God-given vision and calling (see Acts 7:23-25).

Like many modern leaders, Moses had a problem with pride and self-sufficiency. He ran ahead of God, believing that the end justified the means. Moses needed to learn something that many of us need to learn: God wants us to fulfill the purpose for which He created us—but He wants us to fulfill it in His way and according to His timing.

Not only was God less than pleased with Moses' impetuous pursuit of his purpose, when Pharaoh found out, he set out to end Moses' leadership career—permanently. Running for his life, Moses ended up in Midian, about a 150-mile hike across the desert. It was here in the wilderness that God put him through a forty-year rehab program to teach him humility. Moses was still a deliverer, but now he was delivering sheep from predators. This was a big change from his former royal life, but God was preparing him to do things *His* way.

By the time God summoned Moses to Mount Sinai to call him back into active service, Moses had gone from pride to humility to humiliation. During his burning-bush encounter, Moses used every possible excuse to remind God that he was not capable, not equipped, and not equal to the job of deliverer in any way, shape, or form. "Send someone else to do it" was his response.

When God wants us to do something—and He's let us know what that something is—He doesn't look too kindly on complacency. Maybe it was when "God burned with anger" that Moses realized he wasn't going to wiggle out of his assignment.

Well, you know the story. God used Moses to make Pharaoh and his kingdom so utterly miserable that his royal highness finally relented and told the Israelites to pack up, get out, and take whatever they wanted with them. But it didn't take Pharaoh long to regret his decision and call for his army and six hundred chariots to pursue the Israelites, which they did—all the way into the Red Sea.

It's amazing what performing a Red Sea miracle will do for a leader's self-esteem. I imagine Moses was once again feeling pretty good about himself after he and his two-million-plus nomadic community[2] celebrated their victory over Pharaoh's army with songs of praise to God. But his sweet taste of success was short-lived. Three days later the people began to grumble because they were thirsty. And, once again, God used Moses—this time to provide them with water. Then they grumbled because they were hungry, selectively remembering and reminding Moses of their tasty diet back in Egypt. God instructed Moses on how to take care of this problem, too—for forty years.

I admit that by this point in the story I'm feeling sorry for Moses. After a guy has parted large bodies of water by holding out a home-made staff and acted as God's miracle broker, daily feeding a population larger than Manhattan for a really long time, it's hard for me to fault him for giving in to the temptation of thinking he could handle most anything by himself. A few weeks into their journey, Moses did just that. He was once again tempted to assume more responsibility than God intended. But this time Moses' father-in-law and wilderness mentor helped him see the danger of letting his leadership gifts run away with him.

From morning to night Jethro had watched his son-in-law take his seat as the sole judge, trying to solve everyone's problems and disputes. Thinking that one judge could preside over more than two million people may seem odd. But remember, Moses felt responsible. He was their God-appointed leader. What's more, the Israelites looked up to him as their deliverer. In their mind, he alone could lead them into a better future.

This volume of responsibility, authority, and notoriety may stroke a guy's ego, but it's dangerous for everyone involved—including the leader himself. No matter how altruistic a leader's motives may be in the beginning, the magnetism of such power can easily draw him into thinking that it is he, not God, who is master of the universe. It's embarrassing to think about how many times I've let this attitude slip in the back door of my thinking—and it wasn't pretty. I wish I'd had a Jethro in my life to knock some sense into my hard head. Here's what happened in Moses' case.

When Jethro asked Moses why he took on this gargantuan responsibility, note Moses' answer: "Because the people come to me . . ." Can't you just see Jethro shaking his head as he responded with this sage advice? "Moses' father-in-law replied, 'What you are doing is not good. You and these people who come to you will only wear yourselves out. The work is too heavy for you; you cannot handle it alone'" (Exodus 18:15, 17-18).

What was true then is just as true today. When we elevate leadership to the dizzying heights we did at the end of the twentieth century and rely on leaders to solve all our problems, we can also count on negative outcomes. Here are a few to consider.

1. **We fail to give credit where credit is due,** discounting the contribution of others. When we give recognition only to leaders for accomplishments that required a team or community of people to achieve, those who are really responsible for the success are deprived of the rewards and encouragement they deserve. In Moses' case, it's easy to elevate him to superhero status. After all, he had personally talked to God and done some pretty amazing things. But in focusing on Moses, we forget that Aaron, Miriam, and the tribal elders and family leaders assumed responsibility for overseeing the welfare of more than two

million relatives on a long-term camping trip. Bags had to be packed, money raised, bread baked, livestock and provisions gathered. These thousands of responsible men and women were essential to getting all those people out of Egypt and on the road to the Promised Land.

Fifteen hundred years later, the apostle Paul confronted the church at Corinth for their similar tendency to elevate certain people with out-front gifts.

> *Now the body is not made up of one part but of many. If the foot should say, "Because I am not a hand, I do not belong to the body," it would not for that reason cease to be part of the body. And if the ear should say, "Because I am not an eye, I do not belong to the body," it would not for that reason cease to be part of the body. If the whole body were an eye, where would the sense of hearing be? If the whole body were an ear, where would the sense of smell be? But in fact God has arranged the parts in the body, every one of them, just as he wanted them to be. If they were all one part, where would the body be? As it is, there are many parts, but one body.* 1 Corinthians 12:14-20

No one is expendable in the body of Christ. Everyone is essential. Moving a family, community, church, or business toward legitimate achievement of any sort always involves a team of people who take on responsibility. Leaders of every variety must recognize the important part they play, while at the same time giving other responsible people the authority, resources, and affirmation they need and deserve. In other words, a good leader encourages leadership at all levels.

As we move toward the close of the first decade of the twenty-first century, the definition of effective leadership is already morphing from an overemphasis on decisive individual leaders to an approach that is more inclusive of a multitude of gifts.[3] People around the world are realizing that one leader, no matter how gifted, can't possibly have all the skills needed to effectively lead an organization today. In fact, one leader has never had all the skills needed.

Heads of companies make a big mistake when they don't honor and recognize the people who did the work to make their company successful. Recently a guy told me how he and a number of other high-performing individuals had added millions of dollars to their company's bottom line. The president of the company couldn't bring himself to acknowledge their contribution in any significant way. The top-notch sales team who had worked their tails off grew weary of the president taking all the credit for the company's growth when interviewed by the press. And they really got tired of him raising their sales goals without raising their compensation. They finally decided that enough was enough and left en masse to work for another competitor. Today the original company is struggling to survive.

> *The bravest things we do in our lives are usually known only to ourselves. No one throws ticker tape on the man who chooses to be faithful to his wife or the lawyer who didn't take the drug money.*
> PEGGY NOONAN

History makes a pretty good case that if there is any expendable group in God's Kingdom work, it may be the standout leaders. Think about it: When the early church was persecuted, church leaders were forced into hiding in Jerusalem while the other believers scattered, so that the power of the gospel roared across the Mediterranean world like a giant tsunami (see Acts 8:1-2). The message of Christ had to be carried forth by ordinary followers of Jesus. A similar phenomenon happened in twentieth-century China. In the late 1940s, when missionaries were run out of the country and church leaders were forced underground, the Chinese church exploded numerically.

2. **Potential for God's Kingdom work is lost.** When we idolize leaders and place too much stock in their leadership, we begin believing that anything of value must come down from above, according to the chain of command. As for Moses, he came precariously close to taking God's place in the people's eyes. The

Israelites acted as if everything depended upon their leader, and they refused initially to go to their tribal leaders instead of Moses to solve their problems—a problem in and of itself.

Overdependence on one person at the top stifles leadership initiative and resourcefulness at all levels. People become selfishly apathetic and think, *Why should I put myself out, take a risk, or exercise initiative? That's the leader's job.* Surrendering freedom can seem harmless and even attractive when security, a powerful opiate, is offered in its place. And like a narcotic, dependence on leadership is poisonous and addictive to an organization.

Initiative, responsibility, and ownership by all employees are needed for any organization to reach its potential. Yet when a company depends too much on its leader, these essentials are replaced by control, dependence, and an environment in which everyone is looking out for his or her own interests. Valuable talents that God placed within each individual are held in check by the belief that leadership at the top is what makes for success, not the contribution of those lower on the organizational chart.

It's rather disturbing to think that we die for freedom and democracy and celebrate the fall of communism, yet when it comes to our businesses, churches, and communities, we willingly grant leadership power that demands compliance. Looking for leaders who will tell us what to do, give us direction, and set standards for obedience, we often mirror a totalitarian state more than a democracy.

It is unrealistic to think that people will flourish in an organization run in this manner any more than they will flourish in the drab, hopeless mediocrity produced by communist cultures. Leadership goals in command-and-control settings rarely rise above the self-interests of those in charge, and rank-and-file citizens become pawns for achieving them.

Jesus turned this concept of leadership on its head when He responded to James and John's request for positions of leadership and authority in His kingdom.

> *Jesus called them together and said, "You know that those who are regarded as rulers of the Gentiles lord it over them, and their high officials exercise authority over them. Not so with you. Instead, whoever wants to become great among you must be your servant, and whoever wants to be first must be slave of all. For even the Son of Man did not come to be served, but to serve, and to give his life as a ransom for many."* Mark 10:42-45

Please note that Jesus didn't rebuke James and John for their *desire* for positions of leadership; He confronted their *concept* of leadership. He wanted them (and us) to understand that leadership is not about getting others to serve us or our purposes—no matter how noble, right, and good they are. Leadership is about abandoning self-interest to serve those we lead. It's about helping everyone achieve God's purpose.

While not stating this directly, this passage in Mark implies that those being led are not children who need everything done for them. They are people with gifts, abilities, and resources who need to be developed so they can do what God designed them to do, not be exploited by controlling leaders seeking to advance their own interests.

Not too long ago I talked with a pastor who was irate because a member of his church had the audacity to give his time, money, and energy to a non-church-sponsored ministry. In an unguarded moment, the pastor unzipped his heart and revealed his priorities. He wanted his congregation's 100 percent buy-in on *his* agenda, *his* purposes, and *his* vision. It never entered the pastor's mind to help this congregation member pursue the vision and purpose to which God had called him. The pastor's agenda was the only one that mattered.

> **Liberty means responsibility. That's why most men dread it.**
> GEORGE BERNARD SHAW

3. **Leaders get grandiose ideas of their own importance.** When leaders become impressed with their own job description or title and believe that success is the result of their hard work and talent, lower-level leaders and others in the organization become

expendable. This certainly happened to Moses when he first attempted to deliver God's people. Filled with self-importance, the young Moses compulsively struck and killed an Egyptian taskmaster who got in his way.

Feeling indispensable is a modern plague with ancient roots, and every leader is susceptible. Years later, when Jethro realized that the Israelites' overdependence on Moses could tempt him to turn and walk down that familiar path of self-importance once again, he stepped in.

We probably can all name leaders we've known who were so fixated on their God-given vision that they wouldn't let anything or anyone get in the way—even if it meant walking over people, stretching the truth, and abandoning their family like excess baggage. Men like this are vision-focused, not God-focused. This is pretty embarrassing to admit, but I know what it's like to be so caught up in a great cause that you lose touch with reality. I didn't go so far as to physically abandon my family, but at the time I sure thought what I was doing was more important than meeting their needs. Let's call it like it is. That's emotional abandonment.

On the extreme dark side of this tendency, a leader becomes so thoroughly self-absorbed that he bends God's standards for his own indulgence, as if moral standards apply to everyone but him. It becomes easy for anyone in this frame of mind to rationalize that he deserves a reward or a little pleasure because he gives so much to God. King David fell victim to this attitude when he lusted after and slept with the wife of one of his loyal soldiers. Then, in a desperate attempt to cover his sin and her pregnancy, he contrived a plan to have Uriah the Hittite killed in battle.

Jesus had some good advice for leaders who think too highly of their own importance. He told His disciples, "So you also, when you have done everything you were told to do, should say, 'We are unworthy servants; we have only done our duty'" (Luke 17:10). This is a far cry from modern ego-driven leaders who demand outlandish salaries, which is especially de-motivating to the people who actually have to do the work that creates the leader's success.

An Ancient Solution for a Modern Problem

So how does a leader avoid elevating his own importance and minimizing the contribution of others? Jethro gave Moses some excellent advice about how to escape these leadership traps.

> Listen now to me and I will give you some advice, and may God be with you. You must be the people's representative before God and bring their disputes to him. Teach them the decrees and laws, and show them the way to live and the duties they are to perform. But select capable men from all the people—men who fear God, trustworthy men who hate dishonest gain—and appoint them as officials over thousands, hundreds, fifties and tens. Have them serve as judges for the people at all times, but have them bring every difficult case to you; the simple cases they can decide themselves. That will make your load lighter, because they will share it with you. If you do this and God so commands, you will be able to stand the strain, and all these people will go home satisfied. Exodus 18:19-23

Rather than putting all the power in the hands of one leader, Jethro proposed that Moses lead by giving away responsibility and authority. He believed that God can use a lot of people to make good choices. It worked in the desert for Moses. It worked for Jesus when He gave away authority to His followers. It worked in the early church when the apostles gave power away to faithful followers. It works today when leaders release decision-making power and put it into the hands of people actually doing the work.

Booker T. Washington summed it well: "Few things help an individual more than to place responsibility upon him, and to let him know that you trust him." It might be surprising, but that's exactly what God has done for you. Listen to what Paul says in Ephesians 3:20: "Now to him who is able to do immeasurably more than all we ask or imagine, according to his power that is at work *within us* . . ." (emphasis mine).

God has invested gifts, abilities, and talents in every man along with the dreams and imagination to use them. He has entrusted every one of us with His work and the power to get it done—not a privileged few. And as you'll discover in the chapters ahead, that involves a lot more than what goes on at church. God's work involves the meeting of legitimate human needs in the workplace, community, home, and church. Wherever we've been given responsibility—great or small—there is a leadership role to play.

Living as a Faithful Steward

It's time for you and me to stop looking for leaders to solve our problems and start leading right where we are. We need to address life's issues as the leaders God called us to be, taking responsibility and initiative in the decisions set before us. When enough men in any organization—be it a family, church, or company—begin to lead in this way, great things can happen.

Max De Pree, chairman of Herman Miller, Inc., gives us a self-test to assess whether we are doing this. "The signs of outstanding leadership appear primarily among the followers. Are the followers reaching their potential? Are they learning? Serving? Do they achieve the required results? Do they change with grace? Manage conflict?" In other words, *are they leading themselves?*

1. How has this chapter changed your perception of leadership?

2. What areas of responsibility has God entrusted to your care? In other words, where does He expect you to be a leader?

3. Have you ever blamed another leader for something that you should have taken responsibility for? If so, briefly explain.

4. Have you ever been the victim of an egotistical leader? How did it feel? How did you respond?

5. What barriers get in the way of you becoming the leader God intends you to be?

Everyday Leaders

Do not wait for leaders; do it alone, person to person.
MOTHER TERESA

We live in the Age of Quantification. We want to know how many, how much, and for how long. When it comes to leadership, we like to grade skills, measure behaviors, and add up accomplishments. Google "leadership qualifications" and you'll get more than 1.5 million results, including articles like "Eight Characteristics of Leadership," "The Ultimate 21 Traits of Leaders," "Four Key Tests of a Leader," plus countless attribute assessments, personality checklists, and certification tests. Not that these are all bad. If I'm going on a mountain-climbing expedition in the Himalayas, I want to know for certain that the expedition leader has every aptitude and qualification to get me up and back down again.

However, the essence of leadership is broader than possessing certain skills and expertise. It's deeper than what any leadership assessment can reveal. And it's much more profound than being accountable to shareholders to impart vision and reap financial results. Business consultant Peter Block suggests that leadership should be viewed more as stewardship—a philosophy of leadership that's actually been around for thousands of years. It's what I call "everyday leadership." And it's taught throughout the pages of Scripture.

If the term *stewardship* makes you think of sermons you've endured about church budgets and building programs, think again. In the ancient world, stewardship was not a religious term, but rather was one of the key functions of commerce. Almost every business concern had a steward who served somewhat like an ancient chief operating officer, running the daily affairs for the master of the house. Simply put, a steward was someone entrusted with the management of someone else's affairs.

Stewardship means to hold in trust for another. In a business setting, Peter Block defines stewardship as "the willingness to be held accountable for the well-being of the larger organization by operating in service, rather than control, of those around us."[1]

Interestingly, as more and more global enterprises are embracing this "new" concept of leadership, many churches seem to be captive to the 1980s, still holding on to a command-and-control idea of what's expected of a leader. In most of the job descriptions for pastor I've seen, there is more emphasis on vision and authority than stewarding other individuals' talents and developing others to lead. Not that vision is unimportant, but the church seems to be the last to catch up to what the business world has rediscovered—and the Bible clearly teaches.

The Nature of a Man's Leadership

In the Bible, stewardship is the inherent standard to which God calls leaders—whether we're leading a country, business, church committee, community organization, pack of Cub Scouts, our family, or ourselves. Paul's exhortation to Timothy on the topic of leadership selection for the early church is applicable to leaders in all these areas.

> He must manage his own family well and see that his children obey him with proper respect. (If anyone does not know how to manage his own family, how can he take care of God's church?) . . . A deacon must be the husband of but one wife and must manage his children and his household well.
> 1 Timothy 3:4-5, 12

Here Paul describes not only the nature of a man's God-given responsibility but also the scope of his leadership duties—which was a lot broader than leading a church. The word *manage* in verse 4 is *proistemi* in the original Greek text. *Proistemi* is made up of two words: *pro*, which means *before, in front of, over*; and *istemi*, which means *to stand*. So, literally, the word means *to stand before, to rule or lead*. Clearly, Paul is saying that if a man's leadership in his household is dubious, then his leadership elsewhere is suspect. But don't make the mistake that Paul is unleashing self-serving tyrants whose status and import exceeds that of other family members'. While the Bible does call men to lead, nowhere does it indicate that a man's leadership is absolute—or even hint that he is always right. While teaching that men hold a stewardship responsibility to lead their household, the Bible also clearly teaches an equality among family members that was unprecedented in the ancient world, as I will explain in later chapters. There are many times when wise leaders defer to others who are more gifted in certain areas.

The core meaning of *proistemi* conveys the idea that a man should "go first" as an exemplary leader. He doesn't wait for someone else to take responsibility; he takes action himself *to care for, to protect, to govern, to help*—all translations of the word *proistemi*. The word in the strongest sense implies a man's unilateral devotion to his responsibilities as a man accountable to God.

> *God has not called me to be successful; he has called me to be faithful.*
> MOTHER TERESA

Contrary to popular understanding, the opposite of a leader is not a follower. It is a passive spectator—someone who waits for others to take responsibility. Rather than stepping forward, a non-leader steps back. God's idea of being a leader means not waiting for someone to tell you what to do. It means taking the initiative and responsibility to be a faithful steward in God's Kingdom, which we shall see extends to every facet of our public and private life.

The Scope of a Man's Leadership

When Paul talks about family in this passage, he means something entirely different from what we generally think of when we use the word. If you think God is interested only in a man's leadership of his nuclear family, think again. The meaning is much broader. The word translated *family* in 1 Timothy 3:5 is the Greek word *oikos*, which literally means *house* or *household*.

In Greek culture an *oikos* was not just a family group or dwelling but the basic economic unit of the community, and it included everyone who lived in or worked at the house or estate. An *oikos* included immediate and extended family members, slaves, hired servants, skilled workers of various sorts, teachers, and tutors. The influence of an *oikos* extended into the community to those who did business with the household. And if a church happened to meet in a house, the influence of the *oikos* extended to the members of the house church and each of their *oikoi* too.

The Greek word for stewardship, *oikonomia*, is a compound of two words: *oikos*, household, and *nomos*, which means law or rule. In ancient culture, the words used together meant the administration or management of a household. (We get our English word *economy* from this compound word.) The translators of the King James Bible used the English word *steward* to translate *oikonomos*. The New International Version uses more modern terms, such as *manager, management, administering, those entrusted with,* and *those being given a trust*. But none of these English words capture the rich picture of leadership, authority, and accountability that the original Greek words portray.

An *oikonomos*, or steward, was indeed the "ruler of the house," but he was not the ultimate ruler. In fact, in New Testament times the steward was almost always a slave to whom the head of the house entrusted the management of his family and affairs. Although he was a slave, he was second in command, so to speak. He was in authority as well as under authority. But—and this is the point of this Greek lesson—the authority granted to him was never to be used for his own self-interest. He was to use it to advance the interests of the master to whom he was accountable and his master's household.

In the early days of the church when Paul wrote his first letter to Timothy, leadership was expected of every man as he carried out his daily tasks and responsibilities. It was not an abstract concept or a top-level activity of superstars, but could be observed at street level in the everyday activities of the head of the household. Looking at leadership through the lens of stewardship—authority over people and accountability before God—is the key to understanding what it means to lead from a biblical perspective. And leaders who understand and accept this stewardship are desperately needed today in our families, businesses, and communities.

It is this framework for leadership that serves as the backbone of this book. In the chapters that follow we will examine what leadership looks like in the family, in business, in the church, and in the community. It is this *everyday* leadership that we're missing from top to bottom in our culture.

> *Find out where you can render service, and then render it. The rest is up to the Lord.*
> S. S. KRESGE

The diagram below not only provides an outline for the rest of this book, but a picture of each of our responsibilities as a man. First, we must lead ourselves, which means taking responsibility for our relationship with God, our spiritual growth, and our personal development. From that foundation we lead in our families, our workplaces, our communities, and our churches.

As men, you and I have been given resources and relationships in each of these areas for which we have also been given responsibility before God. That responsibility is a stewardship in which we must be found faithful.

The Nature of Steward Leadership

The essence of stewardship implies a two-party proposition. One person owns the resources and the other person is entrusted with the resources. By definition a steward is accountable to his master for how resources are invested. So how does this apply to us today? Since God owns all things, He is the Master; He distributes gifts and resources at His discretion. We are stewards, accountable to Him for all that we do with all that we are given.

To be faithful stewards we must understand four important leadership principles.

1. **The principle of ownership.** A leader has privilege, responsibility, and authority because he has been *given* these by his master. A steward doesn't own; he holds in trust and uses what he has been given for the one who owns it. Arrogance and pride don't have any wiggle room in this equation. The title deed to our lives and the entire universe is in God's name, and He holds all the rights of ownership. An organization—be it a family, company, or church—is not created for the leader, nor is it created by the leader. Everything we have comes from God. The Bible is clear, He owns it all: "The earth is the LORD's, and everything in it, the world, and all who live in it" (Psalm 24:1).

   In response to this divine claim, Abraham Kuyper, prime minister of the Netherlands at the turn of the twentieth century, proclaimed: "There is not one square millimeter of this entire creation about which Jesus Christ does not cry out, 'This is mine! It belongs to me!'" Everything in this world is God's, not only by right of creation, but by right of preservation as well. All that we have added to Creation—the skills and abilities we've used and the raw materials we've developed—are from God. But He knows well the tendency of mankind to claim ownership and take more credit than is due.

   Read His reminder to the Jews before they entered the Promised Land. While the Bible clearly affirms the private ownership of property, Moses reminded the Jews that God is the ultimate owner. "You may say to yourself, 'My power and the strength of my hands have produced this wealth for me.' But remember the LORD your God, for it is he who gives you the ability to produce wealth" (Deuteronomy 8:17-18).

Every individual is also His, not only by right of creation, but also by right of redemption. "Do you not know that your body is a temple of the Holy Spirit, who is in you, whom you have received from God? You are not your own; you were bought at a price. Therefore honor God with your body" (1 Corinthians 6:19-20).

Nothing, not even our very lives, belongs to us in an ultimate sense. As much as we might like to define ourselves by the size of our home, the speed of our car, or our title at work, everything we are and have is God's. As men whom God has called to be leaders, we must be constantly aware that our time, skills, and energy, and every resource, person, and opportunity comes from God. These are not ours to use as we wish, no matter how hard we may have worked and no matter what we have contributed. We are stewards, not owners. I like how C. S. Lewis puts it.

> Every faculty you have, your power of thinking or of moving your limbs from moment to moment, is given you by God. If you devoted every moment of your whole life exclusively to His service you could not give Him anything that was not in a sense His own already. So that when we talk of a man doing anything of God or giving anything to God, I will tell you what it is really like. It is like a small child going to its father and saying, "Daddy, give me sixpence to buy you a birthday present." Of course, the father does, and he is pleased with the child's present. It is all very nice and proper, but only an idiot would think that the father is sixpence to the good on the transaction.[2]

2. **The principle of responsibility.** When I was a college freshman, I borrowed my resident assistant's car to drive a friend and myself on an off-campus errand. To impress my friend, I hit the accelerator when the light turned green and left no small amount of rubber on the pavement. Rather than being impressed, he said to me, "Remind me never to lend you my car."

That was not only a blow to my pride, but a memorable lesson in stewardship. The Bible teaches us that the human race was created to exercise stewardship over our planet. Just like the car I borrowed, it doesn't belong to us. We were given authority and are held responsible as God's stewards for what happens on earth, to the physical world and the people and creatures that dwell here. This is a responsibility that cannot be given or taken away. Whether or not we like it, we are responsible for what God has given. Paul expresses this principle when explaining to the church in Corinth why he preaches the Good News whether he gets paid for his work or not: "If I were doing this on my own initiative, I would deserve payment. But I have no choice, for God has given me this sacred trust" (1 Corinthians 9:17, NLT).

Although God gave us "all things richly to enjoy," nothing is ours. Nothing really belongs to us. God owns everything; we're responsible for how we treat it and what we do with it. While we complain about our *rights* here on earth, the Bible constantly asks, *What about your responsibilities?* Owners have rights; stewards have responsibilities.

Though we don't own anything, God has graciously entrusted us with the care, development, and enjoyment of everything He owns. As His stewards, we are to manage His holdings well and according to His desires and purposes. And it stands to reason that if everything belongs to God, then every decision a leader makes has spiritual implications. Whether we consider something "spiritual" or not, there are no spiritually neutral decisions. Michael Novak puts it like this:

> We didn't give ourselves the personalities, talents, or longings we were born with. When we fulfill these—these gifts from beyond ourselves—it is like fulfilling something we were meant to do. . . . The Creator of all things knows the name of each of us—knows thoroughly, better than we do ourselves, what is in us, for he put it there and intends for us to do something with it—something that meshes with his intentions for many other people. Even if we do not always think of it that

way, each of us was given a calling—by fate, by chance, by destiny, by God. Those who are lucky have found it.[3]

Though we often resist it, most men can grasp the concept of being a steward when it comes to our money and tangible property. But when it comes to taking responsibility for the intangible things, such as our abilities—and especially our relationships—things start getting a little fuzzy.

I have a friend who has done a magnificent job of providing for his family. He has been an excellent steward of his own talent and the financial resources God has given him. However, he often treats family members as if they exist for his convenience. A lot of men tell me they've never considered that they are responsible before God as leaders for the way they deal with others. But they are, and when it comes to people, God is very clear. They belong to Him, not the leader, and they must be led according to His purposes. Every person has been given abilities to serve the purposes of God as He meets the physical, emotional, and spiritual needs of people. In each case stewardship applies. As Peter reminds us, we are each responsible to use our gifts according to God's will. "As each one has received a *special* gift, employ it in serving one another as good stewards of the manifold grace of God" (1 Peter 4:10, NASB).

It follows then, that a man who has responsibility for other people in his home, company, church, or community is not only responsible for using his own gifts for God's purposes, but for how the gifts of those he oversees are used as well. This means that one of our most important responsibilities is to empower the people under our authority to discover, develop, and use the abilities God has given them. This includes our family, those who work with or for us in the workplace, and men and women in the church and community we serve.

3. **The principle of accountability.** As we've learned, when a leader is given responsibility, he is accountable to the one who gave it. Paul reminds us "it is required of stewards that one be

found trustworthy" (1 Corinthians 4:2, NASB). Jesus told several parables in which He used stewardship as metaphor for how His Kingdom operates. Each one ends with the steward giving account of what he had done with the master's property. Each of us is a steward of everything we have been given, including our time, money, abilities, information, wisdom, relationships, and authority. And we will all give account to the rightful Owner as to how well we managed the things He has entrusted to us.

Adam didn't do so well when God called him to account for his behavior in violating His direct command not to eat from a certain tree. True to form, those who want to avoid being held accountable blame others. *She did it.* Or even, *God, it's Your fault.* I don't know about you, but this tendency toward blame runs pretty strong in me and most men I know. When something goes wrong, my default response is to look for someone else to point the finger at. Not that it's always my fault, but that's usually the last place I look. However, personal accountability must be a core value of leaders. Paul reminds us, like it or not, that we too will be held accountable.

> *For we will all stand before God's judgment seat. It is written: " 'As surely as I live,' says the Lord, 'every knee will bow before me; every tongue will confess to God.' " So then, each of us will give an account of himself to God.* Romans 14:10-12

When we stand before God at His judgment seat, He won't be interested in how difficult our wives were to love, how uncooperative our children were to parent, how difficult our boss or employees were to deal with, how obstinate the people were at church, or how corrupt a culture we had to endure. We'll give account for what *we* did with what He gave us. In the chapters ahead, we'll look at both specific actions and attitudes God is looking for from leaders in every area of life.

4. The principle of reward. According to Jesus' parables of the Kingdom, faithful stewards who do the master's will, with the master's resources, can expect a payday. "His master replied,

'Well done, good and faithful servant! You have been faithful with a few things; I will put you in charge of many things. Come and share your master's happiness!'" (Matthew 25:21).

Interestingly, this promise of reward in the New Testament applies not only to the stewards of the huge estates described in Matthew 25, but also to slaves working in a household. Everyone is a steward in God's household and can look forward to a reward for faithful service. Notice what Paul says to slaves in Colossae: "Whatever you do, work at it with all your heart, as working for the Lord, not for men, since you know that you will receive an inheritance from the Lord as a reward. It is the Lord Christ you are serving" (Colossians 3:23-24).

Often a man doesn't consider himself a leader unless he's been given some position of authority in an organization. Yet no matter what level or position you hold, you need to recognize that God has given you some responsibility of leadership—at the very least you are a steward responsible to lead yourself and use your own gifts for His purposes and glory. If you have a family, you have been given a stewardship to lead them well—not for yourself, but for God.

So how do you think you are doing? The Parable of the Talents gives us a clue to the "reward" an unfaithful servant can expect.

> Then the man who had received the one talent came. "Master," he said, "I knew that you are a hard man, harvesting where you have not sown and gathering where you have not scattered seed. So I was afraid and went out and hid your talent in the ground. See, here is what belongs to you." His master replied, "You wicked, lazy servant! So you knew that I harvest where I have not sown and gather where I have not scattered seed? Well then, you should have put my money on deposit with the bankers, so that when I returned I would have received it back with interest. Take the talent from him and give it to the one who has the ten talents. For everyone who has will be given more, and he will have an abundance. Whoever does not have, even what he has will be taken from him. And throw that worthless servant outside, into the

darkness, where there will be weeping and gnashing of teeth." Matthew 25:24-30

This parable is a commentary, not on God's character, but on an unfaithful steward's perception of God's character. If we believe that our Master is harsh and exacting, we will act accordingly. Maybe we won't bury the vast resources that a talent represented (fifteen years' wages), but we will serve our own self-interests, not our Master's. And, in doing so, we will deserve to be thrown "outside, into the darkness, where there will be weeping and gnashing of teeth."

Let's be honest. We know that's what we deserve. I've blown my leadership responsibilities and been less than faithful too many times to count. I've misused my gifts, mishandled finances, mistreated my family, misappropriated praise, and still drive too fast, wasting gas and polluting the environment—but hopefully less than I used to. The good news is that although our Master is an exacting judge, He is also a loving Father. The penalty deserved by faithless stewards was absorbed by the Master's own Son. Jesus, the faithful Steward, received the judgment we deserved. He was thrown outside the Father's household and felt the hellish darkness of separation from His Father for our sake. He offers to exchange His faithfulness for our faithlessness, so we can be welcomed back into His Father's household. As we serve the Master, we need not fear the outer darkness ever again. Look at Paul's amazing statement: "If we are faithless, he will remain faithful, for he cannot disown himself" (2 Timothy 2:13).

Jesus' humiliation on the cross not only removed the fear of ultimate failure, it provided the example of selfless leadership. Jesus proved that He was the ultimate steward, not accumulating power for Himself but giving it away.

Each of you should look not only to your own interests, but also to the interests of others. Your attitude should be the same as that of Christ Jesus: Who, being in very nature God, did not consider equality with God something to be grasped, but made himself nothing, taking the very nature of a servant, being made in human likeness. And being found in appearance as a man, he humbled himself and became obedient to death—even death on a cross! Philippians 2:4-8

Living as a Faithful Steward

To help you clarify where you have responsibilities as a steward-leader, complete the exercises below. If you are working through this book with a small group, talk with one another about what you discovered through this process.

Take inventory. Take a look at each of the realms of stewardship on the chart below.

1. What has God entrusted to your care in each realm?

Get the Master's instructions. If we are responsible to God as our Master, then learning His desires is one of the steward's chief responsibilities. Making decisions that honor Him, as demands a good steward, means knowing His likes, dislikes, vision, and values.

2. Do you know what God expects of you in each area of your life?

Do a preaccountability assessment. Look at each area of responsibility. How are you doing?

3. If you stood before God today and had to give an account, would He tell you, "Well done, good and faithful servant" or something more severe?

Move on from failure. Jesus made it possible for us to lead without fear. If we've made mistakes, there is no reason for those who know

Christ to "bury our talent." Instead we can make the changes we need to make and freely invest all we've been given in the Father's work as faithful stewards.

4. In what areas do you need to claim God's forgiveness and move toward faithfulness? A good start would be to look at the areas where you tend to blame others.

The Leaders God Intended

I need a hero. . . .
He's gotta be sure
And it's gotta be soon
And he's gotta be larger than life
BONNIE TYLER

The lyrics of the song "I Need a Hero" express the unspoken dreams of many women, including those of my wife when we married. Kathy was convinced that I was her "knight in shining armor," able to rescue and protect her from the harsh, cruel world and courageously carry her to Happily Ever Afterville. I'm not sure what I did to sweep her off her feet, but I'm pretty sure it wasn't my dancing. And, as is the case with any woman who is looking for a larger-than-life hero, Kathy found out pretty soon that her dream-come-true was more like a nightmare.

While Sonny and Cher were singing, "They say our love won't pay the rent," Kathy and I got married, believing we could live on love.[1] We each said for richer or poorer, but living below the poverty line (as I pursued my graduate degree) was more than she bargained for. When love couldn't pay the rent, I was "undubbed" knight in shining armor. Between study, work, a new wife, and soon a new baby on the way, I wasn't meeting anyone's expectations—much less Kathy's. I was beginning to think of myself more like a hobbit than a knight.

Like most guys, I've never liked being put in a situation in which there's no way to win. Annoyed, I started wondering where this whole knight-in-shining-armor fantasy thing originated. Maybe, I figured, it was John Wayne who set the rest of us up for failure. I mean, who among us could come close to matching the guy's gallantry. Then I recalled a number of other men in literature and history—Lancelot, Robin Hood, Mark Anthony, Samson, and David, for example—whose strength, skills, and presence caused women to swoon.

But even before these heroes, there once really was a man who was strong, sure, and "larger than life"—at least compared to me and the guys I know. That man was Adam, the first of our species and gender. Adam's godlike presence and authority on earth are remembered not only in the biblical account of Creation, but in yearnings buried deep in the trace of primordial memory found in both men and women today. We instinctively know we were created for something beyond the human experience in the world.

The fact that God gave mankind *dominion over* all creation certainly indicates that God created man to lead. Adam and Eve were conceived in God's mind, designed, gifted, and commissioned to reign as king and queen over the entire earth.

> Then God said, "Let us make man in our image, in our likeness, and let them rule over the fish of the sea and the birds of the air, over the livestock, over all the earth, and over all the creatures that move along the ground." So God created man in his own image, in the image of God he created him; male and female he created them. Genesis 1:26-27

Adam's Job Description in Regards to Creation

God focused more specifically on what Adam and Eve's leadership role would be in the next verse. In what some have called the Cultural Mandate, four commands punctuate Genesis 1:28, setting forth God's intention for mankind.

> God blessed them and said to them, "Be fruitful and increase in number; fill the earth and subdue it. Rule over the fish of the sea and the birds of the air and over every living creature that moves on the ground."

These commands summarize our job description as stewards of the earth and our responsibilities as men.

1. *Be fruitful.* We are commanded to be productive, not just taking and using God's creation, but giving back. He has charged us with the responsibility of developing the raw materials of earth into new and beneficial things. In Genesis 2, God gets more specific: "Now the LORD God had planted a garden in the east, in Eden; and there he put the man he had formed. . . . The LORD God took the man and put him in the Garden of Eden to work it and take care of it" (Genesis 2:8, 15).

    Note the word *work* in verse 15. This is a common Hebrew word that means to *serve*. So, in a sense, the Garden belonged to Adam in that God planted it, then handed it over to him. But in another sense, Adam belonged to the Garden as its developer and protector. In other words, Adam was the first steward bound to the Master's intentions. Adam could not use what God had created in any way he chose. He was to use it according to the will of God, the ultimate owner. And God's will was that it would bear much fruit.

    Also note that Adam did not have a John Deere to help him work the Garden, nor were there tools leaning against the shed awaiting his use. There wasn't even a shed—yet. Everything Adam needed to do his work had to be conceived, designed, invented, and crafted. But he had the resources of all of creation from which to draw, as well as a sharp, unfallen mind to contemplate the development of the first technology.

2. *Increase in number.* We are commanded to multiply, bear children, and populate the earth with new princes and princesses. The work of developing the entire earth was more than two individuals could handle. Adam and Eve needed others to join them in this great adventure. But rather than create more of the human species Himself, God gave Adam and Eve the joy—physically and emotionally—of bringing new creatures just like themselves into the world. That meant, of course, that

relationships, society, and culture would develop. Families, then communities, then regional groups would emerge. Division of labor would emerge based on giftedness and joy in work itself, bringing advances in the arts and technology. And as the human family grew, so would the need for organized leadership if they were to bring their job of stewarding God's creation to its proper end.

3. *Fill the earth.* We are commanded to keep in mind God's goal for His creation. In the original Hebrew text, the idea expressed is not to fill the earth with people through population growth, but to bring the earth—all of God's creation—to maturity, to completion, so that it fulfills its purpose.

   Buried in the DNA of Adam and Eve were all the abilities necessary for them and succeeding generations to fully develop the earth by exploiting (in the best sense of the word) every resource. Human potential and natural resources would combine to create a society and technological advances that would foster a productivity we cannot begin to imagine. Great technological innovations would emerge out of the exuberant expression of mankind's creative potential, not as a result of war. Rather than causing pain and misery, every advance and accomplishment would be a blessing to all of creation.

4. *Subdue it.* We are commanded to bring creation under subjection. The Hebrew word translated *subdue* indicates that this subjugation was to be accomplished by force if necessary. Clearly, God made man a steward in charge of a creation that was wild, untamed, and in need of domestication.

   However, God also gave Adam authority over creation. In the ancient Near East, when one had the power to name something, this implied that he had authority over it. Notice that God held the prerogative to name the parts of His creation in Genesis 1, but He shared that authority with Adam to name the animals God created. He *brought* the animals to Adam to name and delegated that responsibility to Adam as His chosen representative on the earth. In today's vernacular, Adam was tapped and commissioned by God to work as His trusted leader. "Now the LORD God had formed out of the ground all the beasts of the field and all the birds of the air. He brought them to the man to see what he would name them; and whatever the man called each living creature, that was its name" (Genesis 2:19).

Adam carried out these responsibilities with complete, uncontaminated use of all his faculties, spiritually, socially, emotionally, and intellectually. As the leader of God's enterprise on planet Earth, Adam was able to give himself fully to his work and relationships without feelings of inadequacy, fear, or reservation because of his perfect relationship with his Creator.

Adam and Eve's Relationship

Adam's leadership responsibilities encompassed not only the Garden and animals, but Eve as well. However, Adam's leadership of Eve is on an entirely different plane than his authority over the rest of creation. When God charged Adam with naming the animals, He taught him about delegated authority, but He also taught him about the kind of leader he would need to be. Leadership is no solo act. "So the man gave names to all the livestock, the birds of the air and all the beasts of the field. But for Adam no suitable helper was found" (Genesis 2:20).

Through this exercise Adam learned that he was not created to lead alone. As awesome a creature as he was, by design he was not complete. When God delivered his bride, Adam immediately recognized her as his equal in every way: "The man said, 'This is now bone of my bones and flesh of my flesh; she shall be called 'woman,' for she was taken out of man'" (Genesis 2:23).

Eve was Adam's equivalent, his partner. Like Adam, she bore the image of God, and she shared the dominion God granted to humankind through Adam in Genesis 1. They were the monarchs of the entire earth, sharing the fourfold mandate from God.

The leadership pattern that God initiated on earth was relational, not unilateral, and not about one person's superiority over an inferior, but leadership among equals. It was shared, and yet there was a distinct leadership responsibility delegated to the man. This ought not surprise us since mankind was made in God's image, the image of a relational Godhead that shares the leadership of the universe as three in one, each with a unique role to play. But just as there is leadership and role differentiation within the equals of the Trinity, there is leadership and role differentiation within the equals of God's leadership team on earth: "Now I want you to realize that the head of every man is Christ, and the head of the woman is man, and the head of Christ is God" (1 Corinthians 11:3).

What God Did When Adam Led

What was God's response to Adam's leadership? First, He blessed Adam's work. Under God's rule, creation responded to Adam and Eve's work and authority. Under Adam and Eve's hand, the earth flourished. And as a result, there was no scarcity; they had everything they needed in abundance. "And the Lord God made all kinds of trees grow out of the ground—trees that were pleasing to the eye and good for food" (Genesis 2:9).

Although Adam certainly labored, frustration, failed projects, and tedious boredom were unknown in the Garden. The joy of success, a feeling of accomplishment, and a profound sense of purpose filled Adam as he did his work.

Second, God blessed Adam's relationships. Rather than conflict, jealousy, and mistrust that often characterize our relationships, Adam's leadership brought unity, security, and confidence. What an incredible picture Genesis paints: "The man and his wife were both naked, and they felt no shame" (Genesis 2:25).

No wonder God looked at His completed creation and saw that "it was very good" (Genesis 1:31). What does God do when men lead? He blesses our obedience as good stewards.

However, that's only part of the story.

What God Did When Adam Failed to Lead

Genesis 3 follows Genesis 2, and, sadly, we live in another reality today as a result. This new reality is a direct consequence of Adam's failure to lead.

You probably remember the story: Satan, in the form of a serpent, convinced Eve that God was keeping something good from her and Adam by forbidding them from eating from the tree of the knowledge of good and evil. "When the woman saw that the fruit of the tree was good for food and pleasing to the eye, and also desirable for gaining wisdom, she took some and ate it. She also gave some to her husband, who was with her, and he ate it" (Genesis 3:6).

As we read the opening verses of Genesis 3, it's hard not to puzzle over Adam's silence during the conversation between Eve and the serpent. His absence from the dialogue is almost unexplainable. But make no mistake. He was there. When Eve took that fateful bite, the Bible tells us that she gave some to her husband, "who was with her." He didn't step in to protect his wife from Satan's deception. He didn't speak up, contradict, or intervene. He chose to keep his mouth shut, sit passively, and shirk his God-given stewardship to "care for" Eve. He exercised his authority to freely choose, but not for the welfare of his wife and not for God's glory. By failing to act responsibly, he seized God's right to rule as the absolute owner of creation. He was an unfaithful steward.

As much as we men might want to blame women for our current state of affairs, God doesn't. Eve was deceived,[2] and God does not speak of her offense. However, Adam disobeyed knowingly and willingly and God brought the consequence He promised. "To Adam he said, 'Because you listened to your wife and ate . . .'" (Genesis 3:17).

Some mistakenly believe the Bible teaches that men shouldn't listen to women. That's simply not true. Many women's words are filled with wisdom, and as much as we may hate to admit it, we need a woman's perspective to lead wisely. The word *listened* used here means not only to *hear* but to *heed*—not just to consider, but to obey. Adam listened to his wife *instead* of God, and his failure to lead allowed her not only to be deceived but to act on that deception.

When Adam finally opens his mouth to respond to God's direct question, it's apparent the world has drastically changed.

> *He [Adam] answered, "I heard you [God] in the garden, and I was afraid because I was naked; so I hid." And he said, "Who told you that you were naked? Have you eaten from the tree that I commanded you not to eat from?" The man said, "The woman you put here with me—she gave me some fruit from the tree, and I ate it."* Genesis 3:10-12

Instead of security there is fear; instead of dignity there is shame; and instead of leadership there is blame. Passed down from that first generation to the next, this heritage of passivity still plagues us today, resulting in broken homes, broken businesses, broken communities, and broken churches. Every day, passive men refuse to turn off the television when they know the program content is harmful to their children. Men who know better participate in—or refuse to confront—unethical business dealings instead of standing up for what is right. They feel spiritual when they warm a pew and drop a twenty in the plate. They drive past community trouble spots, blaming politicians for the big problems while neglecting to make even the small contribution that could make a difference.

The Nature of the Curse

Rather than the blessing and reward due a faithful steward, man's failure to lead brought disharmony, desperation, and death to himself, his wife, and the planet on which we dwell. Adam's inaction impacted not only the human race but the entire physical world. The curse shows us what God does when men *don't* lead.

> *To the woman he said, "I will greatly increase your pains in childbearing; with pain you will give birth to children. Your desire will be for your husband, and he will rule over you."*
> *To Adam he said, "Because you listened to your wife and ate from the tree about which I commanded you, 'You must not eat of it,' [c]ursed is the ground because of you; through painful toil you will eat of it all the days of your life. It will produce thorns and thistles for you, and you will eat the plants of the field. By the sweat of your brow you will eat your food until you return*

to the ground, since from it you were taken; for dust you are and to dust you will return." Genesis 3:16-19

Through Adam's inaction, disharmony was sown into the human heart, and leadership, especially in the family, became a proverbial problem. For the woman, not only did child-birth become painful, but so did living with the man it took to bear the children. Gone forever was the trusting abandonment of her welfare to her God-appointed leader. He had failed her and then blamed and betrayed her. Why would she ever put trust in men again? She had to be strong; she had to protect herself. The phrase "Your desire will be for your husband" means the desire for control, understandably motivated by the desire for the security and safety Eve craved that her man no longer provided. Now women are born into the world naturally suspicious of men, and we confirm their misgivings by our actions and attitudes. And sadly, our selfish passivity on one hand and domineering hubris on the other only reinforce women's suspicion that we are simply not safe.

> *Having been made in the image of God, man is magnificent even in ruin.*
> FRANCIS SCHAEFFER

Hollywood has humorized and capitalized on how men sometimes go to great extremes trying to win a woman's trust. In the hit movie *Hitch*, Will Smith plays a consultant who makes his living helping clients trick women into giving them a chance to prove they are different than other men. Such stories aren't quite as funny to women who live in the reality of relationships with men who can't be trusted. The irony of tricking women to trust a man is no laughing matter in real life.

To make things worse, women's attitudes reinforce our greatest angst as men—that we're *not enough*. Of course, that fear is well founded. We were never enough to run the world independently apart from God. To paraphrase C. S. Lewis in *The Great Divorce*, when Adam failed to say, "Thy will be done" to God, God said "Thy will be done" to man. In other words, "Run the world on your own"— something we will never be able to do successfully.

Adam's failure to lead had led to a multisystem breakdown. God in His wisdom allowed the natural consequence of Adam's choice to fall as judgment on His rebellious steward. But that consequence is not only judgment, it is an act of grace, a constant reminder that allows every generation of men to experience what it is like to live alone without God.

It's hard to imagine the shock to the system that spiritual death must have had on Adam and Eve. To have experienced the utter perfection and beauty of their bodies' dazzling spiritual oneness with God must have been magnificent. Then to be left with the hulking emptiness of a spiritually vacated body must have been similar to the repulsion a person feels when gazing on the deformed, decaying lifelessness of a corpse. No wonder Adam and Eve wanted to cover themselves!

Plus, for Adam and Eve to have gone from a world in which everything they tried to accomplish "worked" to a world that refused to cooperate must have been excruciatingly painful. With all its wonder and beauty, the world we have inherited from our first parents is far from friendly, and even farther from reliable.

New Day, Same Job

Though conditions since the Garden have changed drastically, two things have not: God still holds us responsible to lead as His stewards, and He promises to reward our faithfulness. As we have seen, the key to faithful stewardship is to *discern* what the owner wants and then *do* what that owner wants. A steward is bound to his master's agenda. Far from limiting our freedom as Eve was tempted to believe, the agenda of an all-wise, all-good, all-powerful Creator—who wants to do the very best thing for you, me, and all creation—sets us free. And when we freely choose to be faithful to the stewardship He has entrusted to us, God promises to reward us.

Jesus describes this final account in the Parable of the Talents in Matthew 25. Rather than fearing this time of accountability, the faithful steward has only joy and the ultimate significance—Christ's commendation—to look forward to. "His master replied, 'Well done, good and faithful servant! You have been faithful with a few things; I will put you in charge of many things. Come and share your master's happiness!'" (Matthew 25:21)

God's Reality Check

But don't misunderstand God's blessing and make the mistake of thinking that somehow we can manipulate God into making the world work right for us when we reject passivity. In other words, don't think that if we do what's right, we can expect God to make our life comfortable and painless. The effects of the Fall are unavoidable, even for faithful stewards. Job is a biblical example of this reality. Although he was incredibly wealthy—and by God's standards, blameless—he suffered great relational, financial, and personal loss and pain.

You and I see the evidence of this reality today. Being a godly, faithful man doesn't guarantee that a wife will be faithful in return. Being ethical doesn't guarantee success in your work. Walking with Jesus doesn't lead to a pain-free life. One of the most faithful men I know lost two sons within a year and a half, both boys within months of their twenty-first birthday.

Try as we might, we can't outdistance the broken condition of the fallen world this side of heaven. Jesus led well, never embraced passivity, and still experienced rejection, hatred, abuse, and injustice. There is no magic wand Christians can wave over their lives to ensure the outcome they want.

The book of Ecclesiastes is the Bible's reality check. When we start thinking that we can just work a little harder, act a little smarter, gain a little more experience, and make life work the way we want it to, Ecclesiastes reminds us that the world, as it is currently managed, guarantees us nothing.

This sobering book affirms that the world is God's creation, filled with good gifts given for us to enjoy, but reminds us that the results of the Fall on life is *futility*. The Hebrew word means "transitory, empty, fleeting." Even the good gifts of God are unstable, unsteady, and unreliable—nothing on which to build your life, nowhere to find solid footing or sink a firm foundation. The term does not imply that life is meaningless, pointless, or worthless. Good gifts we receive in this world can and should be enjoyed, but wisdom demands that we ought never to stake our lives on anything, even God's good gifts—since all are unreliable. Ultimately they will not satisfy. There is nothing stable enough to build our life upon apart from God Himself. And when we try to make life work without Him we can expect selfishness, blame, hatred, prejudice, and condescension to undermine our relationships and our work.

Hope for a Fallen World

The consequence of Adam's failure to lead colors everything in life with futility and instability. And yet, the redemptive power of Jesus Christ gives men and women who trust Him the source of security and adequacy, love and significance that allow us to move beyond the futility of this world. Although we live in a fallen world and are subject to the same frustration, pain, and futility of life that even Christ faced, our restored relationship with the Creator and the stability it brings give us the resources to transcend the cycle of failure and become the leaders we were meant to be.

> *God created the world out of nothing, and so long as we are nothing, He can make something out of us.*
> MARTIN LUTHER

Our inadequacy is transformed to adequacy: "I can do everything through him [Christ] who gives me strength" (Philippians 4:13). Our insecurity is transformed to security: "For I am convinced that neither death nor life, neither angels nor demons, neither the present nor the future, nor any powers, neither height nor depth, nor anything else in all creation, will be able to separate us from the love of God that is in Christ Jesus our Lord" (Romans 8:38-39).

When we understand that our adequacy and significance come through our right relationship with God through Christ, we are set free from the quicksand of trying to prove ourselves and are released to be the leaders God intended. And when we are faithful to our leadership responsibility, we can expect the blessing God promises to faithful stewards. As leaders step back under God's authority and say, "Thy will be done," the inner healing we experience delivers healing to our family, our work, our church, and our community.

While we cannot re-create the perfect world of the Garden, we can do more than pray "Thy Kingdom come." We can do our best to make the environments in which we live reflect the Garden's environment as much as possible. For example, we can assume our responsibility to love and serve our wives and children unconditionally. We can do our work diligently and for God's glory, not ours. We can treat people fairly and with the respect they deserve as men and women created in the image of God. We can steward the environment wisely and resist abuse. We can lead courageously in our churches and communities. We can do this by taking responsibility for the one thing we do control: ourselves.

Living as a Faithful Steward

Our faithfulness as men reminds people that this fallen world is not all there is. Our faithfulness makes it easier for our spouses, children, friends, and coworkers to choose faithfulness as well. God uses our responsible stewardship to make Himself known in a world that has been blinded to and is oblivious to His presence. This is what God does when men lead.

1. Think about your daily work. How has the Fall impacted your work?

2. Think about your relationships. How has the Fall impacted them? What would they be like if the Fall had never occurred?

3. How has the Fall affected your ability to lead as a man? Is the biggest problem internally in you or externally in the world?

4. Where are you experiencing the impact of the Fall most painfully in your life?

5. Think about standing before God and giving an account as His steward. What would be the most fulfilling thing He could say to you?

6. Name one thing you can do to make your life reflect the Garden reality of a perfect relationship with God.

PART TWO

LEADING YOURSELF

Those who can command themselves command others.
WILLIAM HAZLITT, British essayist

Not the maker of plans and promises, but rather the one who offers faithful service in small matters. This is the person who is most likely to achieve what is good and lasting.
GOETHE

Do not pray for easy lives. Pray to be stronger men. Do not pray for tasks equal to your powers. Pray for powers equal to your tasks.
PHILLIPS BROOKS

CHAPTER 4

Following the Real Leader

You don't understand. I could have had class. I could have been a contender. I could have been somebody, instead of a bum—which is what I am.   MALLOY in *On the Waterfront*

Every man I know, including myself, wants to be somebody. We want to make a difference in the world and know that our life matters. We want to leave our mark on others so that when we are gone, people will remember us for the contribution we made. Men long for that immortality. We erect buildings, build businesses, write books, and seek fame so we will be known while alive and remembered when we are gone.

When his obituary ran in the newspaper prematurely, Alfred Nobel, the inventor of dynamite, learned that he would be immortalized as the "merchant of death." Determined to be remembered for something positive, he left the bulk of his estate to fund the Nobel Prize. Today, over one hundred years after his death, he is remembered for the Nobel Prize, not as an arms manufacturer. Though most of us don't have the means to mount that kind of posthumous PR campaign, we all want "to be a contender" in one way or another.

I believe this longing to make our mark is God-designed and stems from an ancient, subliminal understanding of our true identity given in the Garden of Eden. Passed down through numberless generations from fathers to sons, it lingers in our minds as an undeniable compulsion to matter and contribute to creation.

It is here, at this longing, that the curse fell on the male of our species. As a result of Adam's sin, this God-given desire to work has been twisted so that we instinctively seek to self-define our significance through what we do, apart from God. Since the first man, Adam, acted independently from God and decided, *my* will, instead of *Thy* will, be done, things on earth have never been the same.

Although the Bible does not provide details, I imagine that before the Fall, whatever Adam put his hand to proved successful. He planted and grew crops without having to worry about pests destroying them. When he confronted wild animals, they submitted. As he ruled over all of creation, it cooperated with him. Being absolutely accepted by God, he had no need to "prove" himself adequate. He instinctively knew his significance. When Adam had the ability we all want—to prove he was somebody—he had no need to do so.

However, due to mankind's rebellion, creation no longer "works" for us or with us and regularly reminds us of our inadequacy apart from God. And it is precisely at this point of frustration that leadership begins. Before we lead others, we must learn to lead ourselves. Before we can lead ourselves, we have to face this truth: We can never be the somebody we want to be, apart from God.

Becoming a Somebody in a Nameless World

The mandate to subdue the earth that God embedded in our being as men became an affliction to us after the Fall. Since then, as much as we strive and connive to rule over creation—as well as ourselves—it never works. In fact, it never will, short of Christ's return to put all of creation under His rule once again.

The pain and frustration we experience from our inability and failure to control the world has a purpose—and that purpose is for our good. As C. S. Lewis said, "God whispers to us in our pleasures, speaks in our conscience, but shouts in our pains: it is His megaphone to rouse a deaf world."[1] Pain and frustration, day in and day out, prevent us from ever reaching a self-satisfied state that would anesthetize us from realizing our need of God. This deep desire to rule, to make a name for ourselves and make a difference in the world, can never be realized apart from God. And the frustration we experience in our efforts to do so apart from Him is a gift of His grace meant to drive us back to Him.

Yet we try our best to ignore our pain. Although we continue to fail, we persist on exploiting creation and using our God-given ingenuity to quench our appetite to rule and make a name for ourselves on our own terms. One way we do this is by comparing ourselves to and seeking to distinguish ourselves from others. When we are able to gain authority over others, win over an opponent, or accumulate more "trophies" or wealth than the next man, we experience a wisp of victory in our attempt to define ourselves by comparison. But it will always be a short-lived victory and leave us with the nagging thought that it might not go so well the next time. There is always someone—younger, faster, smarter, better—ready to snatch our hard-won name from us.

In his autobiography, *Quiet Strength*, Tony Dungy, coach of the 2007 Super Bowl champions, the Indianapolis Colts, relates how he came to grips with this. During his third year as an NFL player, Dungy was sidelined in preseason by an illness. He became frustrated when he realized he might be unable to play that season. Then teammate Donnie Shell confronted him: "Tony, I think you are at a crossroads. You know what life is all about. You profess to be a Christian, and you tell everybody that God has first place in your life. Now, when your career looks like it's teetering, we're getting a chance to see what *really* is in first place for you. . . . All the Lord is trying to do is find out what's first place in your life, and right now, it looks like football is."

After some serious soul-searching, Dungy realized Shell was right. Dungy says, "It was the first time I was able to look at football as something that God was allowing me to do, not something that should define me. I couldn't take my identity from this sport; I had to consciously make sure that God was in first place."[2]

When Dungy stood on the podium to receive the Super Bowl XLI trophy for his team's victory over the Chicago Bears, it was apparent that his victory wasn't about making a name for himself. Though he enjoyed the success, it didn't define him. God did.

Dungy tells us what was on his mind on game day, "The Super Bowl is great, but it's not the greatest thing. My focus over the last two weeks leading up to the Super Bowl was Matthew 16:26, in which Jesus asks, 'And what do you benefit if you gain the whole world but lose your own soul?'" (NLT)[3]

Theologians like me could stand to learn a lot from godly NFL coaches. I was sad and humiliated when God pointed out this desire to define myself on my terms a few years ago. I was speaking before an audience (with great authority, I might add) from Colossians 3. As I heard my own amplified voice saying, "We go to work to make a name for God, not to make a name for ourselves," the Holy Spirit's presence and grip on my heart was palpable. With great shame I realized that beneath the surface of my ministry was a motivation to prove myself. I could hardly finish my message because of my grief over this personal failure. Here I was, supposedly working for God, and suddenly I realized how much I was working to define myself on my terms. No wonder I had been miffed over the lack of respect a colleague showed me. No wonder I was angry that someone else had undermined my influence. No wonder I felt proud knowing I worked harder than anyone else. I was busy building an image of who I wanted to be. Fortunately God graciously convicted me before I caused more damage to myself or others.

> Don't rejoice in successful service, but rejoice because you are richly related to Christ.
>
> OSWALD CHAMBERS

Because I am a sinful man, I know this tendency to make a name for myself (which is nothing less than crafting an image of myself that I hope people will worship) is something that will haunt me the rest of my life. Seeking satisfaction from popularity, power, and prestige is as addictive as cocaine. It is my "drug" of choice, as it is for many men.

Ironically, though, when we seek satisfaction or desire anything more than God, that desire becomes a curse, separating us from the only One who can satisfy. In Romans 1:24 (NASB) Paul says, "God gave them over in the lusts of their hearts." Don't think that lust simply means wishing you could sleep with your neighbor's wife. Doing good—when it's sought as a substitute for God—can get us into trouble too. If God had given me the acclaim, power, and prestige that I desired, it would have taken me down the road of pride and self-sufficiency. And any of us who travel this road are headed for an unwelcome destination—one that brings pain, not only to ourselves, but to those we love as well.

I'm glad to know I'm not the only self-seeking jerk in the world. Even Jesus' disciples had moments of self-grandeur. The twelve guys from the backwater province of Galilee didn't seem like overly ambitious types—the kind who would want to run the world. But hanging around powerful people can inflate any guy's ego.

For example, in Mark 8:29 we read that the disciples clearly understood that Jesus was their long-awaited Messiah. Speaking for the entire group, Peter tells Jesus who they think He is: "You are the Christ." This declaration marked a significant shift in Jesus' ministry. Jesus was quick to clarify that this name came from God the Father, not Peter. "Jesus replied, 'Blessed are you, Simon son of Jonah, for this was not revealed to you by man, but by my Father in heaven'" (Matthew 16:17).

Like any good leader, Jesus then began to both clarify His mission and prepare His disciples for what lay ahead. Imagine their alarm when Jesus informed them that the road to His throne was by way of the Cross—think torturous execution. Forgetting himself in the shock of the moment at this unpleasant news, Peter took it upon himself to rebuke Jesus in the strongest language possible and to correct His vision of the future.

Peter's reproach of Jesus stemmed not only from an incomplete view of Jesus' mission but from his own pride. He assumed authority he hadn't been given. By recognizing who Jesus was, Peter thought he had named Jesus, and as we have seen, naming implies authority over the named. It is ironic that receiving insight and revelation often makes people proud rather than humble. Truth isn't discovered, defined, or constructed by human beings. It's revealed to us. Sadly, we want to claim credit for something we were given.

It's easy to critique Peter's response, but consider how you might feel as a top executive on the CEO of the world's leadership team. Instead of a seven-figure salary, six weeks of vacation, and use of the company jet, you're told to expect to be maligned, mistreated, and rejected. Grounds for indignation in anyone's book, wouldn't you agree? Suffering and death were not what Peter or any of the disciples signed up for. From boyhood, they had each learned and held firmly to a committed expectation that the Messiah would come to His throne, usher in His Kingdom, and end suffering and injustice. Nope, suffering was not part of any of the disciples' vision of their immediate future.

God had a different plan. In order to achieve the greatest leadership turnaround of all time—end Satan's enslavement of the human race and free all creation from the curse—Jesus was headed to Jerusalem, not to seize power but to lose it. He was going not to rule, but to serve. "He then began to teach them that the Son of Man must suffer many things and be rejected by the elders, chief priests and teachers of the law, and that he must be killed and after three days rise again" (Mark 8:31).

Note that Jesus did not outline one of a number of possible plans. He told them that the Son of Man *must* suffer. It was absolutely necessary. There was no Plan B, no shortcut or way around the cross. The accomplishment of His mission to offer pardon to the human race, defeat evil, and populate His kingdom in the future demanded that He become a servant choosing to suffer in our place. There was no other path.

But it wasn't just Peter who had exaggerated ideas of his own importance. His two former fishing partners, James and John, decided that they wanted to be in the top positions of leadership in God's kingdom and sit on Jesus' right and left when He came to the throne (see Mark 10:35-37). When the other disciples heard this, they showed their true colors too. It seems that all of them were focused on their future privilege and authority. Mark tells us, "When the ten heard about this, they became indignant with James and John" (Mark 10:41). But note that Jesus does not rebuke them for desiring positions of leadership. He does, however, correct their understanding of leadership in His kingdom.

> *Jesus called them together and said, "You know that those who are regarded as rulers of the Gentiles lord it over them, and their high officials exercise authority over them. Not so with you. Instead, whoever wants to become great among you must be your servant, and whoever wants to be first must be slave of all. For even the Son of Man did not come to be served, but to serve, and to give his life as a ransom for many."* Mark 10:42-45

Here Jesus outlines what kingdom leadership entails and authenticates it by His own life and leadership style. In so many words, Jesus said that if you want to be a great leader, then you should follow His example. His leadership sets the standard.

Following the Leader

What does all of this mean to you and me? Fortunately, Jesus did not leave it to us to figure out. For those who wish to follow Him, three changes are required.

1. Following Christ means a change in a leader's agenda. I used to wonder how Peter could proclaim that he believed Jesus was the Messiah and the Son of God one day and shortly thereafter rebuke Jesus as he would a demon from hell. Then I realized that I often respond with the same attitude when some unexpected turn of events or negative circumstance doesn't match my expectation of what God should be doing.

As 2006 came to a close, I breathed a sigh of relief and thanked God for getting my wife, Kathy, and me through one of the toughest years of our lives. I was exhausted and felt like I had to crawl across the annual finish line. Two weeks later Kathy was diagnosed with breast cancer. Trust me, my first response after the initial shock was not: *How is this going to make us more like Christ and bring God glory?* Rather than responding in faith, my mind was filled with doubt. I know that life is filled with pain. I know if Jesus suffered, my family and I will suffer. I'm willing to take a lot, but I complained, "Lord, this feels like You're piling on."

When I compared my response to Peter's, I could see what was going on. Like most men, when I have an agenda and someone—even God—gets in my way, I am put out. In my case, I was ready for an easier year. In Peter's case, he expected to be somebody. For both of us, Jesus—or rather what we expected Him to do for us—was our ticket to security and significance. Giving up something this important is tough for a man.

Those of us who want to follow Jesus must constantly check our expectations (and make necessary adjustments) to make sure we're not using Jesus just to bring about our own agenda, whatever that might be. Following Jesus is about getting on *His* agenda. But if you are like Peter and me, you had certain expectations when you aligned yourself with Christ—although you probably didn't prenegotiate your "deal" with Him beforehand.

> *What comes to mind when we think of God is the most important thing about us.*
>
> A. W. TOZER

Now down the road, we discover that this is costing a lot more than we bargained for and the path is not leading where we wanted to go—or at least it is not taking us as fast as we expected to get there. We may experience a lot more pain than pleasure and more humiliation than recognition. It's easy to start wondering, *Is this worth it?* We start thinking that we'd like to renegotiate our deal, only to find that this is always a nonstarter with God. After all, He is God. But this doesn't stop us from shaking our fist, giving Him what we think is good advice, or just flat giving up trying. When we get into this mind-set, we need to ask ourselves some tough questions: How have I come to regard God as someone I can manipulate? How have I come to think I'm smarter than God about what needs to happen? How can I even compare what I've sacrificed for Him to what He sacrificed for me?

When the disciples' hopes were dashed, Jesus gave them new hope. He showed them a larger reality. True, He was going to die. But that was not the end of the story. His route to the throne was through the Cross, but it was that route that would ultimately open the Kingdom of God and bring them more joy and status—even in their most selfish moments—than they ever dreamed possible. He gave them a Kingdom perspective: "I tell you the truth, some who are standing here will not taste death before they see the kingdom of God come with power" (Mark 9:1).

And note that hope is not in circumstances, but in a person.

Trusting Christ does not necessarily make painful experiences hurt less. It does, however, make them mean something different. They may hurt us, but they cannot harm us. When Kathy got the news about her cancer, I was eight thousand miles away in Birmingham, England. I had learned that the radiologist had signaled a problem a few days before as I was leaving for the airport. But we had faith and prayed for a positive report. All that prayer and faith didn't change the fact that cancer was growing in her body. Now the reality hit.

I felt as hopeless and helpless as I've ever felt in my life. I also felt guilty for having left Kathy, as if my presence would have brought a different outcome. A wave of fear washed over my mind at the thought of living one day without my beloved. Fortunately some dear friends were in the next room praying. They gathered around me when I told them the news. They gave me a Kingdom perspective, reminding me that Kathy was safer in God's hands than she was in mine and that He was in control—that I wasn't and never had been. I don't think it made it hurt less, but it made it hurt differently, in a way I can't quite describe at this point in this journey. The helplessness did not abate, but the hopelessness gave way to trust in God's sovereign goodness.

The next six months included four surgeries and a lot of unknowns. Until we got the good news about Kathy's prognosis, I had to deal with the reality that God's purposes and my desire for Kathy's healing might be at counterpurposes. I constantly had to remind myself that my hope was in God, not in what I wanted Him to do for me. The reality was that I might have to face my worst nightmare—for Kathy to face a painful death and for me to lose this woman who is so much a part of my life. I wasn't sure how I could face that. But I also knew that there is no pain without the promise of reward, an eternal weight of glory that Paul reminds us will make the pain seem trite in comparison (see 2 Corinthians 4:13-18).

2. **Following Christ means a change in a leader's value system.**
After rebuking Peter, Jesus made an important point very clear. He summoned the nearby crowd and told them, along with His disciples, that there is a cost to discipleship.

> *If anyone would come after me, he must deny himself and take up his cross and follow me. For whoever wants to save his life will lose it, but whoever loses his life for me and for the gospel will save it. What good is it for a man to gain the whole world, yet forfeit his soul? Or what can a man give in exchange for his soul?* Mark 8:34-37

These oft-quoted words of Jesus communicate a profound truth that no man who wants to follow Christ and be an effective leader can afford to miss. Jesus' words may have puzzled His disciples, but not in the same way they sometimes puzzle us. Those who listened would have known that Jesus was not talking about eternal life or physical life. They would have understood that He was not promising eternal life to martyrs, nor was He tying salvation to obedience. The Greek word Mark uses for *life* here is *psyche*.[4] Psyche, which is often translated *soul*, is the word from which we get our word *psychology*. It refers not to the immortal soul, but to a man's individual self—his identity and personality that distinguishes his life from others. In this passage *psyche* is used as a synonym for the personal pronoun *he*, paralleling "deny *himself*."

Here's what Jesus was getting at. Every man comes into this world suffering from an identity crisis. Separated from God, he doesn't know who he is, yet the drive to distinguish himself is so strong, it controls his life. For the most part, Eastern religions have rightly recognized this drive as one of the most destructive forces on earth, keeping men captive in darkness. Yet they propose the wrong solution. According to their thinking, the path to enlightenment is not the road to find oneself, but to eradicate self entirely—to be absorbed into oneness with the universe, losing one's individual identity. In other words, you *are* a nobody—so get over it.

In contrast, Western philosophy and culture have sought to help people find satisfaction and fill their identity vacuum by elevating certain values. For instance, they tell us that if we gain this or achieve that, we will be somebody. Conventional culture tells us we're nobody without a family and children. Our own individualistic consumer culture stresses personal achievement— we're somebody based on the level of power and position we attain and the number of possessions we accumulate.

Interestingly, however, there is a common denominator to both Eastern and Western approaches: We're told our identity and significance as individuals are based on something we gain from the world.

Jesus doesn't tell us to drive our need for identity underground; He wants us to find our true identity, our true sense of self, which can come only from Him. We can't acquire it no matter how much we try; it's a gift. It's not from this world; it's from Him. What we must crucify is not our longing to know we are somebody but our commitment to obtain our identity from the world apart from God. If you have ever tried to let go of something you have used to define yourself, you know why Jesus says it's like going to the cross. It feels like an execution because it is. It's something we think we need to live. When we turn something by which we have defined ourselves loose, the person who we think we are dies—and needs to die so that we can discover our true selves. It's hard to hold our hands out to receive a gift when we are clutching something else with all our might.

If you've never lost your job, I highly recommend it. Getting fired is even better. Not that I'm advocating bad behavior, but sometimes men are fired because they chose to stand on principle, despite the potential cost. They should take their dismissal as a compliment. Nonetheless, no matter what the reason for being let go, nothing is more unsettling to a man than to have his work rejected. I know this from experience. Sitting on the other side of gainful employment is a life-rearranging experience. Since I, like other men, have a tendency to define myself by what I do, cleaning out my desk and walking into the ranks of the unemployed rates as one of the most difficult things I've done in my life. On the other hand, I must add that it resulted in the most significant spiritual growth, giving me the opportunity to find my real identity in Christ.

It doesn't matter if it's a job, a relationship, a house, a bank account, or your reputation. Jesus says that holding on to it for dear life will cause you to lose sight of your real identity, the only thing that can make you a somebody. Clutching possessions won't work. Gain the whole world and you still won't have a solid self. It's futility, remember. Sure, you'll have stuff, but not a life. No matter how much you achieve, no matter how much you earn, it will never be enough to make you sure—really sure—that you are somebody. The accumulation of every treasure in the world is not enough to satisfy the need for identity of one human being. It's like being afloat on the ocean without a drop of fresh water. Even though you have water in every direction to drink, it will not satisfy your thirst. Only Jesus can do that.

3. **Following Christ means a change in a leader's trajectory.**
Whatever else it means, becoming a leader means first and foremost that we must lead ourselves to line up right behind Jesus. Each of us must first choose to lead ourselves to become a servant. According to Jesus, the way up is down. This counterintuitive trajectory was as hard for the disciples to swallow as

it is for us. Leadership is not essentially about power, author-ity, vision, respect, or even influence—not that these things lack leadership significance. But leadership is primarily about sacrifice and servanthood. It's about the direction of the leader's heart, not the power he holds in his hand. Paul reminds us in Philippians 2 that our "attitude should be the same as that of Christ Jesus" (v. 5).

> *Who, being in very nature God, did not consider equality with God something to be grasped, but made himself nothing, taking the very nature of a servant, being made in human likeness. And being found in appearance as a man, he humbled himself and became obedient to death—even death on a cross! Therefore God exalted him to the highest place and gave him the name that is above every name, that at the name of Jesus every knee should bow, in heaven and on earth and under the earth, and every tongue confess that Jesus Christ is Lord, to the glory of God the Father.* Philippians 2:6-11

In not seeking to hold on to His name, Jesus was given a name above all others.

Boss, president, prime minister, CEO, king. These are all coveted titles men fight to claim and keep, but the name that means something, the name that is solid, significant, and lasting is not the name we earn, but the name we are given by God. That name can only be known by those who hold these other names lightly, and who are willing to throw their worldly status to the wind and give themselves away in sacrificial service to the One who gave Himself for them.

Living as a Faithful Steward

As you think about what you've read in this chapter, don't miss the parallel between what Adam lost and what Christ has restored. We rejected God's will in the Garden (Eden) and lost our *name*. Jesus accepted God's will in the garden (Gethsemane) and gained a *name* for Himself—and for us. He had a true identity and was a some-body, but chose to give up His status for our sake so that we could gain a true identity and become the somebodies He created us to be. If our identity is secure in Jesus, we have nothing to lose by giving ourselves away as faithful stewards, and everything to gain.

1. What did you think life would be like when you trusted Christ? Is following Jesus costing more than you bargained for? Has it been worth it?

2. Is your identity strong enough to hold up under the loss of your job, title, work?

3. As you examine your life, what is it about your agendas, values, and trajectory that needs to change?

4. Is your hope in Jesus or in what you expect Him to do for you? What needs to "die" in your life?

5. If you're the master, it all depends on you. If you're the steward, it all depends on the Master. What freedom can this bring you?

CHAPTER 5

Don't Miss Your Calling

Most of us have jobs that are too small for our spirit. Jobs are not big enough for people.   STUDS TERKEL

I hope you are beginning to think of yourself as a steward and leader of God's creation on earth. It is a high and noble calling for the Master of the universe to entrust you and me with such responsibility. Yet perhaps you're puzzled because you aren't sure of the precise arena in which God wants you to lead—and exactly over what He wants you to be a steward. Few of us are called to shoulder the responsibilities of leading countries, military forces, or Fortune 500 companies—which causes some of us to breathe a sigh of relief. For others the thought of taking on vast leadership responsibilities is invigorating. It all depends on how God has gifted and called you.

At one time or another, most of us struggle with knowing God's purpose for our lives and what part of His creation He wants us to lead. We want to know, *Why do I exist? Where do I fit in? What do I have to offer this world? What is my purpose?* But for all who ask, few seem to find a satisfying answer. We can understand why people who do not know Christ as their Creator, Redeemer, and purpose-giver should puzzle over their purpose. But it stands to reason that Christians should have a clearer picture of what God wants them to do with their lives. Yet many Christians think discovering God's will is a little like the quest to find the Holy Grail. They spend their lives searching for some assurance that they are fulfilling their purpose, all the while not really sure it can be found in the first place. Most wander through life with the vague notion that there must be something more, all the while wishing they were doing something else.

It is at this point that my own calling kicks in because I love to help people discover their calling. When I told my friend Steve about a study I was leading that could help him clarify what God wanted him to do with his life, he jumped at the chance to participate. Earlier that year a series of events had caused him to begin to ask what he should be doing with his life. First, the title company where he worked was put up for sale, which put his job in jeopardy. Second, he came face-to-face with the less-than-ideal learning environment the students in his twelfth-grade Sunday school class were enduring at their high school. Third, he had the opportunity to visit Eton, one of the premier boarding schools in Great Britain. The lack of such great educational options in his community stirred Steve's soul, but what should he do? His job situation was shaky. Should he make a career change to teaching?

As my group studied what God's Word had to say about calling, uncovered their unique giftedness, and dreamed about what God might do with their life, that "something" Steve should be doing slowly drifted into the realm of his consciousness. (By the way, I'll walk you through this same self-discovery process in the next chapter.) When Steve told the group what God was putting in his heart, I had to control an inclination to smile. You see, Steve wanted to see a New England–style prep school in East Texas—not a place that tends to value that caliber of educational excellence.

Steve decided to buy the company he worked for, which in a few years provided the seed capital for his dream. In 1997, Brook Hill School opened its doors on a sprawling, 180-acre campus just outside Tyler, Texas. Today it offers over four hundred students a Christ-centered, college preparatory education.

That same study group included a thirty-two-year-old schoolteacher. Ann felt the same passion for education that Steve did, but God led her in an entirely different direction. She decided she wanted to work within the local school system and shyly told us she might like to run for the school board. She felt she could bring a fresh voice to public education. Again I wanted to smile. Our community was very provincial in its thinking, and although she sought an elected position, few of those unknown to the community's leaders as the *right* candidates ever won elections. But Ann was convinced God was leading her. Ann stepped out on her dream and resigned her teaching position so she would be eligible to run. Then to her surprise, people began to line up and write checks for her campaign. She won the election and brought the fresh perspective of a classroom teacher to the school board—something sorely missing in the past.

A couple of years ago I met Eric at an election-eve party. As we chatted over hors d'oeuvres, I discovered three things about this successful man. He was good at what he did—financial investments; he was serious about Jesus; and he was confused and frustrated by how these two worlds fit together and was considering a career change. After having subsequent conversations and reading my book *Going Public with Your Faith*, Eric began to see that his clients were his mission field. Eric didn't need a job change, he needed a new vision for how what he was doing already fit into God's plan for his life.

Perhaps you feel as if you've been casting about in vain for your purpose for years. You may doubt that God really has a specific plan for your life. Although at times you may wonder about God's interest in the rumblings and yearnings deep within you, be assured He does have a purpose for your life and that He is not playing games with you. God's purposes for your life and mine are not buried in some faraway place that requires

> *Most people go to the grave with their music still inside them.*
> OLIVER WENDELL HOLMES

an arduous, lifelong quest to uncover. Believe me, God is much more interested in our discovering and doing His will than we are in finding it: "I will lead the blind by ways they have not known, along unfamiliar paths I will guide them; I will turn the darkness into light before them and make the rough places smooth. These are the things I will do; I will not forsake them" (Isaiah 42:16).

Sometimes I meet people who seem blind to their calling. That was the case with Jim, a physician I got to know while working with Christian doctors. Jim was highly intelligent and managed his medical practice well. There was just one problem: He really didn't like seeing patients. As we talked I discovered that he was a fourth-generation doctor. Everyone in his family assumed he would follow the family tradition. His intelligence and work ethic kept him going through medical school and the first years of his practice. But by his forties, his interests in systems and data distracted him from his work with patients. I was able to encourage Jim to consider a move to hospital administration. At first this seemed like a nonoption. After all, he had spent so many years in training and besides, what would his family think. A year later when the hospital where he practiced offered to send him for an MBA in hospital administration, he knew it was the right choice. Today, he loves his work and is able to make a unique contribution in health care because of his training in both business and medicine.

There are two common reasons that men such as Jim have so much trouble discovering the reason for their being. First, Satan is constantly trying to blind and confuse us, his end goal being to blunt our contribution to the furtherance of God's Kingdom.

Although God gives us the ability to resist Satan's antics, we cannot change the way he works. Since Satan cannot snatch God's children from Christ's hand, his only recourse is to thwart our potential for impact. Confusing us and blinding us to our purpose will always be key weapons in his arsenal to keep us from fulfilling God's design for our lives.

A second reason we men have trouble connecting with our calling is that we look in the wrong places and seek the wrong kind of guidance. We make decisions based on what our culture tells us is important. We choose life paths based on earning potential, what our parents or friends advise, or what looks to be the path of least resistance. That's not to say that any of these elements is wrong in and of itself or that God doesn't sometimes use one of these criteria to guide us. But looking to anyone or any circumstance to discern God's will without commiting to know Him and do His will in His way is a setup for taking the wrong path. Fortunately, God offers us a way out of that confusion.

Men of Destiny

God has made His calling and purposes for our lives very clear in the pages of the Old and New Testaments. While we're often primarily concerned with God's specific purpose for our life, before we discover that, we must become aware of His purposes for all His people.

1. God calls us to know Him in a personal and intimate way. God is not some detached deity who created the world and then withdrew His presence. He is a person, and as such He desires a personal relationship with His creatures. Not just fellowship, but a deep, intimate love relationship between creature and Creator, modeled by His relationship with Adam. Sin's devastating effect on the human race at the Fall interrupted this idyllic relationship, but God has opened the door again for that kind of relationship through Christ.

> *Therefore, if anyone is in Christ, he is a new creation; the old has gone, the new has come! All this is from God, who reconciled us to himself through Christ and gave us the ministry of reconciliation: that God was reconciling the world to himself in Christ, not counting men's sins against them. And he has committed to us the message of reconciliation.*
> 2 Corinthians 5:17-19

God created a corresponding longing for intimacy in every human heart. Augustine said, "You have made us for yourself O God, And the heart of man is restless until it finds rest in You." For those who love God, knowing Him is the most compelling longing in their heart. You can almost hear Paul's passion in these verses:

> *I want to know Christ and the power of his resurrection and the fellowship of sharing in his sufferings, becoming like him in his death, and so, somehow, to attain to the resurrection from the dead. Not that I have already obtained all this, or have already been made perfect, but I press on to take hold of*

that for which Christ Jesus took hold of me. Brothers, I do not consider myself yet to have taken hold of it. But one thing I do: Forgetting what is behind and straining toward what is ahead, I press on toward the goal to win the prize for which God has called me heavenward in Christ Jesus. Philippians 3:10-14

God has promised that those who seek Him with all their heart will find Him and know Him.

2. **God calls us to submit to His authority and be conformed to His image.** Because God is the Creator and sustainer of all, knowing Him demands a response of submission. Many people have not yet acknowledged His authority, but someday every person will: "At the name of Jesus every knee should bow" (Philippians 2:10)

Furthermore, when the human race rebelled against God's authority, sin marred the image of God in every human being. But God loves His children too much to leave us in that condition. He is reshaping our character to be like Christ's.

And we know that in all things God works for the good of those who love him, who have been called according to his purpose. For those God foreknew he also predestined to be conformed to the likeness of his Son, that he might be the firstborn among many brothers. Romans 8:28-29

As we grow in our knowledge of Christ, the Holy Spirit works in us to restore His image. He is gradually conforming our character to be like Christ's. "But we all, with unveiled face, beholding as in a mirror the glory of the Lord, are being transformed into the same image from glory to glory, just as from the Lord, the Spirit" (2 Corinthians 3:18, NASB).

As we recognize more of Christ's character being formed in us, we begin to understand that God deserves to occupy the place in our hearts that He occupies in the universe: Lord of all. The desire to run our own lives is replaced by a submission to God's authority over our lives—and until we reach this point, it is difficult (if not impossible) to discover His reasons for creating us.

3. **God calls us to be involved in His work.** While God wants all men to know Him intimately, submit to His authority, and be conformed to His image, He also has a particular purpose for each of us. This is our individual stewardship responsibility on earth. Although we live in a fallen world, God has called us to take and reclaim territory held by the enemy and to be involved in the redemption of all creation, each of us with a specific task to accomplish. "For we are God's workmanship, created in Christ Jesus to do good works, which God prepared in advance for us to do" (Ephesians 2:10).

Certainly, we are to prioritize our own spiritual growth. But if we spend all our time preoccupied with the personal dimension of our relationship with God, we will miss a huge part of God's will for our lives. We are called to *do* as well as *be*. These two aspects of the Christian life are inseparable. What we are to *be* is clear. What we are to *do*, however, is sometimes cloudy.

A Confusing Dichotomy

Perhaps you are wondering, *What are the works God created me to do? What is God's will for me? Is there any way for me to know for certain that I am doing what He called me to do?* These are good questions to ask because if God is who He is, then knowing what His will is should be our top priority, and spending time on anything other than what He thinks is important is not a worthy pursuit.

As you seek to discover God's will for your life, start by examining what you know to be God's will—a worthy ambition for every Christian. Next, don't limit yourself or God. God's interests are very broad.

> *What we really need to have is the Guide himself. Maps, road signs, a few useful phrases are good things, but infinitely better is someone who has been there before and knows the way.*
> ELISABETH ELLIOT

Years ago I heard a man tell about his decision to change majors in college based on the assumption that temporal things are ultimately valueless. He had been studying civil engineering; a natural choice because ever since he was a child, he had loved building things. He had always dreamed of building bridges and highways. Then one day he read 2 Peter 3:10, "But the day of the Lord will come like a thief. The heavens will disappear with a roar; the elements will be destroyed by fire, and the earth and everything in it will be laid bare." As he read this verse, a troubling thought came to his mind: *I'm going to build bridges only for the Lord to come along and burn them up.* All of a sudden, his degree path and career choice seemed like a waste of time. So he decided to go to seminary and become a minister. I'm sad to say many men have made a choice such as this, only to learn later that God wanted their business to be their ministry and they didn't have to give up what they truly loved to do.

Unfortunately, Christians often draw a distinction between "God's work," which they see as having eternal value, and "the world's work," which they believe has only temporal value. Maybe you, like me, learned in church that only two things are eternal: the Word of God and the souls of men. Everything else is of little interest to God. The implication is that if you spend your time and energy on anything other than these two pursuits, you are wasting your time as far as God is concerned.

But is this religious-sounding outlook biblical? Stop for a moment to consider what wonderful blessings roads and bridges are to God's people—before they burn up, that is. Think about all the people who work to meet legitimate human needs—farmers, grocers, truck drivers, home builders. Could it be that God's interests extend a lot further than just the spiritual welfare of His people? As we have seen in Genesis 1 and 2, they do.

Just because worldly thinking dominates the work world does not mean that God is not interested in what's going on outside the walls of the church. The fact is God's work includes a whole variety of activities—spiritual, physical, and emotional. And He wants us to dream about meeting legitimate human needs in all of these areas. Whether we are building bridges or building people, God wants us to do all things for His glory. We'll look at this passage later in more detail, but in Paul's letter to the Christians in Colosse, he says that our daily work ought to be done as an act of worship. "And whatever you do, whether in word or deed, do it all in the name of the Lord Jesus, giving thanks to God the Father through him" (Colossians 3:17).

Those individuals who insist on dividing up the world into the secular versus the sacred forget that 75 percent of the men and women we consider biblical heroes are people who "wasted their time" working in secular jobs most of their lives. In fact, if these divisionists are right, then Jesus Himself wasted the vast majority of His life wielding a hammer as a carpenter.

What makes something sacred or secular, valuable or worthless, pleasing or unpleasing to God, has much more to do with our attitude and motive. We can make any job sacred or secular. Look at Colossians 3 again. It is immaterial to God whether a person manages or is managed, owns or is owned, or is a pastor or a painter. All of us must live by the same rules. We all are to do our work, no matter what it is, for the same reasons we go to church: to worship and glorify God, and serve our fellow man.

If this is the first time you've thought about *all* work being God's work, you may feel as though your life just got more complicated. After all, a whole new realm of possibilities for doing God's will has opened up. While we can rejoice in the breadth of our choices, we still need a way to discern what God has in mind for each of us specifically. In the next chapter we'll look at some tried and true ways to narrow down the field—a way to say *yes* with conviction and *no* without guilt to the myriad opportunities and needs we see in our world. But before we move on, let me tell you a brief story.

According to historian John Pollock, the abolition of the British slave trade was "the greatest moral achievement of the British people."[1] But the man behind the crusade almost missed his calling. When William Wilberforce, the young English member of Parliament, came to Christ at age twenty-five in 1785, he visited John Newton, the old slave-trader-turned-pastor, to seek God's will for his life. Thinking God was more interested in religion than politics, Wilberforce thought he should leave Parliament and take up ministry.

Newton disagreed, suggesting that God might have him in Parliament for a reason. "It is hoped," Newton wrote, "that the Lord has raised you up for the good of the nation."[2] Indeed he had. In 1787 Wilberforce was asked to propose legislation that would abolish the slave trade. He had not sought out this cause. Should he take on the unpopular fight that could predictably cost him his position and potentially his wealth? In his day only a few thought the slave trade evil, and most thought its abolition would bring economic ruin to the empire.

Wilberforce's investigation of the slave trade drove him inexorably to one conclusion: It must be stopped. On Sunday, October 28, 1787, Wilberforce wrote these words in his journal: "God Almighty has set before me two great objects, the suppression of the Slave Trade and the reformation of Manners."[3] How had he come to this conclusion, this calling that would so impact not just his nation, but also the western world? God had laid a burden on his heart he dared not resist. Later he would tell the House of Commons, "So enormous, so dreadful, so irremediable did the Trade's wickedness appear that my own mind was completely made up for Abolition. Let the consequences be what they would, I from this time determined that I would never rest until I had effected its abolition."[4] That passion would last for almost fifty years until not just the slave trade but slavery was abolished in the British Empire.

Is God interested in government, politics, debates, and economics? What about the sweat of a laborer's brow or the way an employer treats his workers? If not, we can place the Bible on the shelf with every other religious text. Over and over again, the Bible says God is interested in the world in which we live. And He has called you to something significant while here. Your life matters. It may not affect nations, but it can bring grace to other people's lives. Don't miss God's calling for your life. Author Nancy Pearcey sums it up well when she writes:

> The ideal human existence is not eternal leisure or an
> endless vacation—or even a monastic retreat into prayer and

meditation—but creative effort expended for the glory of God and the benefit of others. Our calling is not just to "go to heaven" but also to cultivate the earth, not just to "save souls" but also to serve God through our work. For God Himself is engaged not only in the work of salvation but also in the work of preserving and developing His creation. When we obey the Cultural Mandate, we participate in the work of God Himself, as agents of His common grace.[5]

Living as a Faithful Steward

Has Satan tried to confuse you about your calling by limiting your vision about what truly interests God? Don't forget, we can make any job secular by a self-serving attitude, but when a job is done for God's glory, we can bless the world with His grace.

1. How do most people you know choose their work?

2. How did you come to choose your current work? Do you think it is what God wants you to do?

3. How have you defined "working for God" in the past? Do you need to adjust your viewpoint?

4. How does your work serve the common good of men and women? Do you think God is interested in what you do? Why or why not?

5. Read Colossians 3:17 again. What about your current work would change if you did it for God?

Discovering
Your Destiny

It is not revolutions and upheavals that clear the road to new
and better days but . . . someone's soul, inspirited and ablaze.
BORIS PASTERNAK

No matter how gifted or ungifted you think you might be, you have a
destiny and God wants you to know what it is. Destiny is not something reserved for the famous or fabulously gifted. Destiny means
that you have been designed for a purpose. Discovering your destiny is anything but a novel pursuit of self-actualization. It is a critical
aspect of stewardship. Peter reminds us: "As each one has received a
special gift, employ it in serving one another as good stewards of the
manifold grace of God" (1 Peter 4:10, NASB, emphasis mine).

One way to look at destiny is the right person doing the right
thing at the right time. For you personally, this means that your destiny lies at the nexus of three overlapping circles: your gifts, your
passions, and your circumstances.

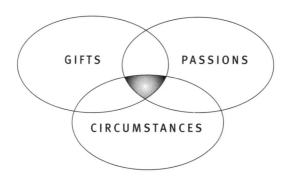

GIFTS   PASSIONS

CIRCUMSTANCES

In this paradigm, gifts determine whether you're the right person for a particular job: Do you have the abilities to do the job well? Passions determine whether you're doing the right thing with those gifts: Do you feel strongly that what you are trying to accomplish is an important undertaking? Circumstances determine whether it's the right time: Has God opened the door of opportunity to make it possible? To discover your destiny, you'll need to take a look at each of these components.

Gifts: What Am I Good At?

Everyone is gifted, but not everyone is gifted in the same way. Contrary to the American maxim that says we can become anything we want to be, we are not blank slates to be written on or lumps of clay molded by ourselves or by forces around us. We come into the world predesigned with a set of God-given abilities bestowed for His purposes.

He gives us natural gifts when we are born and spiritual gifts when we are born again. All of our gifts—both natural and spiritual—are God-ordained, given to us by divine design. They are not acquired nor distributed arbitrarily. They were bestowed so that we might have the capability to achieve certain specific accomplishments God had in mind before we were created. Since God gives these abilities, they come with a responsibility to Him for their use. They themselves are a stewardship. According to Romans 12 our gifts are our calling. It is God's will for us to function in the areas of our God-given strengths.

> *For by the grace given me I say to every one of you: Do not think of yourself more highly than you ought, but rather think of yourself with sober judgment, in accordance with the measure of faith God has given you. Just as each of us has one body with many members, and these members do not all have the same function, so in Christ we who are many form one body, and each member belongs to all the others. We have different gifts, according to the grace given us. If a man's gift is prophesying, let him use it in proportion to his faith. If it is serving, let him serve; if it is teaching, let him teach; if it is*

*encouraging, let him encourage; if it is contributing to the
needs of others, let him give generously; if it is leadership, let
him govern diligently; if it is showing mercy, let him do it
cheerfully.* Romans 12:3-8

Identifying your unique giftedness takes away a great deal of the
guilt and gut-wrenching guesswork of determining God's will for
your life. Every day we are bombarded with expectations from our
friends, parents, spouse, children, coworkers, as well as our church,
our kids' schools, and society as a whole. Identifying and embracing
our God-given gifts and abilities helps us know how God expects
us to respond to these demands. Bundled in your personal array of
gifts is a blueprint of God's intention for how He wants you to invest
your life. To make decisions based only on needs and appeals for
your resources—whether your time, money, energy, or intellect—is
to let people squeeze you into the wrong mold.

Romans 12 also warns us not to take on major commitments un-
supported by our gifts—no matter who is doing the asking. Part of
not being squeezed into the world's mold demands that we say no to
what we're not gifted and graced to do, so we will have the time and
energy to do what we are called to do.

For example, if you like the idea of working with people on a team
or committee but feel challenged when it comes to numbers, don't
be sucked into a job on the church finance committee. If you're good
with numbers but have never been comfortable around small children, it's probably not God who is asking for a year's commitment to
teach the four-year-old Sunday school class. Give yourself and the
kids a break. Say no. If you dislike yard work and are not good when
it comes to house repairs, don't let a Homer Handyman put you on
a guilt trip for not having a perfect yard and home. On the other
hand, if you love any of these tasks, do your work with all vigor and
enthusiasm, knowing that real significance comes from doing what
God gifted you to do.

Fulfillment does not come from pursuing society's (or even your
church's) definition of success. If you are good at making money
and love the business world, understand that your primary place

of ministry is the workplace. You will not find vocational ministry to be a more satisfying place to operate—because the Lord did not make a mistake when He was distributing gifts.

He is a wise man who wastes no energy on the pursuits for which he is not fitted.
GLADSTONE

Using the gifts God gave you brings joy, energy, and enthusiasm. When you function in the area of your God-given abilities, you engage God's creative power, and there is no deeper satisfaction than doing what He desires. Our being knows this intuitively and responds in joy. God designed each of us to play an important role in His Kingdom, and we simply cannot function with any degree of effectiveness outside of that role. His energy flows through the gifts He gave you—not someone else's idea of what you should be doing with yourself.

So what is the best way to confirm your gifts? Follow the scent of joy. It will lead you to the role God designed you to play, the role in which you will feel the greatest sense of satisfaction and enjoyment, and know the greatest effectiveness for the cause of Christ. In the classic movie *Chariots of Fire*, Olympic runner Eric Liddell tells his sister, who was trying to discourage his athletic ambitions, "God made me fast. And when I run I feel His pleasure." You can begin to identify the elements of your design by asking yourself, *When do I feel God's pleasure?* Think of several instances where you experienced a great deal of personal satisfaction in what you have done, and then ask and answer these questions about each instance.

1. What was I doing specifically?
2. How was I going about doing it?
3. What was I using to accomplish what I did?
4. What were the circumstances?
5. Did I work alone or with others? If others, how did I work with them?
6. What was so satisfying about what I did?

When you discover that you've jotted down similar answers repeatedly from instance to instance, you are picking up a pattern of your giftedness. Write them down and use them when you're evaluating any job you take on, whether in a company, the church, or in the community.[1]

Passions: What Do I Feel Strongly About?

Knowing what you're designed to do is only part of the destiny equation. Knowing how to sort through all of the needs, requests, and opportunities presented to you is another part. Maybe your church wants you to head up a new urban ministry. Your boss wants you to oversee a new IT project. Your wife wants you to coach your son's Little League team. Some friends suggest that you run for public office. Assuming you possess the right gifts to do these jobs well, should you take them on? Not necessarily. Don't misunderstand—I'm not suggesting that you bail out of family or work responsibilities. But all of us need a way to assess opportunities and be able to say yes with conviction and no without guilt to requests that come our way. For example, how did William Wilberforce, even after deciding not to quit parliament, know that he was to take on the slave trade as opposed to one of the many other pressing needs of his time?

As I've looked at history and studied Scripture, I've discovered something akin to a North Star for navigating the opportunities and needs that come our way. God has given us an internal compass, and that compass is the passion that is given to guide us to God's will for our lives. The word *passion*, however, is often misunderstood. To some, the word brings back memories of an illicit rendezvous with a high school flame. To others it evokes images of rage. And it is true, passion is behind a lot of sinfulness. Remember what James tells us about passion (or "evil desire," as it's translated here)? "But each one is tempted when, by his own evil desire, he is dragged away and enticed" (James 1:14).

Actually, the concept of passion is morally neutral as far as the Bible is concerned. When our passions or longings attach themselves to sinful objects, the Bible calls them lusts or evil desires. However, passions and deep longings can also attach themselves to ideas and actions that are good. When they do, we need to stop and ask God if this is something He wants us to pursue. Remember Wilberforce's example? The more he studied the slave trade, the heavier the burden became. Eventually he resolved, "Let the consequences be what they would, I from this time determined that I would never rest until I had effected its abolition."[2] That's passion.

Passion is a heartfelt burden, a persistent and powerful emotional response to a need or opportunity. Don't make the mistake of thinking that passion is always focused on righting some dreadful wrong. Passion can focus on seizing some great opportunity as well. It is a God-given ability to feel so deeply about something that it causes you to move toward the object of desire—to meet a need, fight for a cause, undertake an opportunity, right a wrong—to make the world a better place.

> *Without passion man is a mere latent force and possibility, like the flint which awaits the shock of the iron before it can give forth its spark.*
> HENRI-FRÉDÉRIC AMIEL

Unlike gifts, which God permanently bestows but which need development, passions arise at what might seem like arbitrary times in our lives. Their timing is anything but random, however. God in His providence works in our heart, and at the right time He guides us toward our destiny.

Take Nehemiah, for example. As a high official in the palace of the Persian king, he had reached the summit of success in his world. God, however, upset his comfortable life with news from Jerusalem.

> *In the month of Kislev in the twentieth year, while I was in the citadel of Susa, Hanani, one of my brothers, came from Judah with some other men, and I questioned them about the Jewish remnant that survived the exile, and also about Jerusalem. They said to me, "Those who survived the exile and are back in the province are in great trouble and disgrace. The wall of Jerusalem is broken down, and its gates have been burned with fire."*
> Nehemiah 1:1-3

I'm sure a number of people heard the news about Jerusalem upon Hanani's return, but it cut Nehemiah to the quick. God had created a clear path for this news to come straight into Nehemiah's heart. Here's how he responded: "When I heard these things, I sat down and wept. For some days I mourned and fasted and prayed before the God of heaven" (Nehemiah 1:4). That's passion.

My wife, Kathy, says that passion is like a beach ball. You can push it down under the water, but it keeps popping back up. That's what happened to Nehemiah. As much as he might have liked to put this news out of his mind, God kept bringing it up. Read through this great story in the Bible and you'll see that he actually fasted and prayed for several months before God opened the door for him to do something about it.

Nehemiah was a gifted leader. Wilberforce was a gifted politician. But how were they to know how God wanted to invest their gifts? God moves everyone a little differently, but passions play an important place in our lives in leading us to where God wants us to invest our lives. Think of it this way. Knowing our gifts tells us what ammunition we have; our passions tell us the target. They give us direction and keep us off rabbit trails. Also, as a passion begins to burden us, it makes us aware of resources we never before recognized. It may even bring out gifts we may never have discovered. And most of all, it makes us radically dependent on God.

Use the following questions to help you think about what passion God has been laying on your heart. And keep in mind, this is not a one-time exercise.

1. When I lie awake at night, what do I think about when I'm staring at the ceiling? What makes me weep? What makes me want to pound the table?
2. What kind of issues, needs, opportunities, activities, or ideas really motivate me and seem to give me energy?
3. If I could meet any need in the world, had every resource I needed, and knew I could not fail, what would I attempt to do? What need would I attempt to meet? Whom do I most want to help? What opportunity would I want to seize?

When you've finished, summarize and make a list of your strongest passions. Then, prioritize them as best you can and commit them to prayer. Ask God how He wants you to respond. As you pray, listen for what He might reveal as a next step. As Nehemiah prayed, God slowly began to reveal to him that he was going to be the key player in answering his own prayer for Jerusalem. Long before Nehemiah ever got permission from the king to rebuild the walls of Jerusalem, his passion blossomed into a fully flowered dream. And in pursuit of this dream, he began to plan and prepare for the day when he would go to Jerusalem.

Circumstances: Has God Opened a Door?

Without a doubt, waiting on God when a burden has landed and a dream taken flight in our hearts is one of the most difficult parts of pursuing our destiny. Waiting is not something I do well. Once I follow a passion and begin to dream about what God might do, I'm more than ready to take off. My impatience when the door does not open is also an indication of my pride and independent spirit. And this is one of the main reasons God imposes this last component of destiny.

Remember Moses? The guy who murdered the Egyptian trying to follow God's will for his life? Right person: He had all the gifts and training for leadership of a country. Right task: He was passionate about delivering the Jews from bondage. Wrong timing: Moses took matters into his own hands. He wouldn't wait to fulfill his destiny, and it cost him forty years of his life. As a result, an entire generation of his people never knew the exhilarating taste of freedom. It never helps to rehearse *what ifs*, but we can certainly learn from Moses' mistakes. Waiting on God accomplishes a number of important things in our lives.

Waiting settles the ownership issue. When we sense God moving in our heart, we are often tempted to run ahead of God. Unfortunately, it's possible to make a dream from God our master, rather than God Himself. A dream can actually become the driving force of our life, more important than anything else. There's a huge danger as Christ reminds us: "No one can serve two masters. Either he will hate the one and love the other, or he will be devoted to the one and despise the other" (Matthew 6:24).

According to this passage, making our dream more important than God will drive us to despise God. The drive to accomplish the dream will be more important than pleasing Him, more important than doing things His way, and more important than our relationship with Him. We'll despise Him because He's not working on *our* schedule or perhaps is even standing in our way.

Waiting forces us to put what we want to do back in God's hands. Because I'm stubborn, this kind of surrender usually takes time. I don't know about you, but I'm not sure I could count the times that God has had to bring me to the point of desperation as I've relentlessly followed my dream. I've finally had to give up on doing what I wanted to do and say, "Lord, if You want this to take place, then You bring it about. It's Yours. I give up." Often, we must come to this place of despair and surrender before God will move ahead and open the door of opportunity for us. When we wait, we remind ourselves and give testimony to God that the dream belongs to Him, not us. This not only puts us back on the right path, it puts us in a position where God can bless us.

Waiting removes the failure issue. If it's God's dream, then He's the Master responsible for its fulfillment. I'm merely the servant; I'm His tool, responsible to be obedient. The most important thing is not whether I get to do what I want to do. What does matter is that I am a faithful steward in pursuing the opportunity and using everything I can to serve God.

Don't misunderstand. No emotionally healthy man likes to fail. This attitude toward waiting doesn't necessarily make failure less painful, but it does ensure that failure is not fatal. If this is truly God's dream, ultimately, it's His responsibility to fulfill it. Far from removing the drive, this kind of freedom allows us to throw ourselves into God's will with reckless abandon just like the two faithful stewards in the Parable of the Talents in Matthew 25. We have nothing to lose with no fear of failure. The only failure would be to refuse to pursue what God wants for us.

Waiting ensures strength in the stretch. Ironically, waiting not only keeps us from running ahead of God but it allows us to confidently move forward once He opens a door. If the opportunity opens up too quickly and easily without much initial opposition, there's a tremendous temptation to second guess when adversity rears its ugly head. When problems arise, we're tempted to think we've made a mistake thinking, *We've run ahead of God.* A mistake many Christians make is interpreting God's will through the circumstances that surround them at the moment. When things are going our way, this doesn't necessarily mean that we're doing God's will any more than adversity means that we're out of God's will. But when God has clearly opened a door for us to proceed, we can see adversity for what it is—Satan's attempt to discourage and divert us.

When we wait and watch God's hand moving in the affairs of our lives, removing obstacles we could not move and opening doors of opportunity we could not open, we know that we didn't get to where we are on our own. God put us here like a turtle on a fence post, as a friend of mine likes to say. In other words, when you see a turtle on a fence post, you know he didn't get there himself. Someone put him there. If God opened the door for us, He's still with us when things get hard. And that's all that matters, even in the toughest of circumstances.

Perseverance is a hard pill to swallow, but God often prescribes it for our spiritual health. He desires our success even more than we do, so if He can wait, so can we. Proverbs 21:1 reminds us of an important fact: "The king's heart is in the hand of the LORD; he directs it like a watercourse wherever he pleases."

God directs the king, the president, the governor, mayor, employer, the spouse, the parent—anyone in authority over us—and He can open doors and close doors any time He wishes. Wait on Him.

An Important Warning

As you think about clarifying your calling through your gifts, passions, and circumstances, the following three principles will keep you from being sidetracked.

1. **We are bound to keep some obligations, gifted or not.** Countless voices call to us, asking us to respond. In order to ferret out which ones God wants us to respond, you'll want to look at your gifts, passions, and circumstances. However, there are compelling responsibilities that each one of us has to other members of the body of Christ irregardless of our gifts. James reminds us: "What good is it, my brothers, if a man claims to have faith but has no deeds? . . . . Suppose a brother or sister is without clothes and daily food. If one of you says to him, 'Go, I wish you well; keep warm and well fed,' but does nothing about his physical needs, what good is it?" (James 2:14-16).

> *The strength of a man consists in finding out the way God is going and going that way.*
> HENRY WARD BEECHER

   If a brother has a legitimate immediate need and I have the means to meet that need, then I have an obligation to help him on a short-term basis. I don't need to pray about it or seek God's will about it; I just need to obey and do it.

   In any setting—family, work, church, neighborhood—there will be things that must be done that no one wants to do. As in the case of the brother in need, I can't say, "That's not my gift." These tasks must be shared by everyone. In our family, for instance, no one likes to clean the kitchen—although we do like to eat. But if we want to maintain a healthy, sanitary environment, it's got to be done so we all pitch in and do it.

2. **We should say *no* to some opportunities.** Some individuals are highly motivated to meet people's needs. They turn on the TV and hear an appeal to feed the children in Africa. Then they surf to another channel where someone else is requesting funds for

hurricane relief. Later they may get a letter asking for donations for medical research. They want to write a check to them all—even though their bare-bones family budgets can't handle it. For these people, responding compulsively rather than intentionally to needs is a real temptation. Guilt and the need for approval are both unmerciful taskmasters to this kind of person. They disguise themselves well, because their expression of servanthood looks so spiritual.

3. **God has not called us to meet every need.** Each of us has an important part to play, but none of us is called to do everything on our own. Seeking to meet every need not only robs someone else of an opportunity, saying yes to one opportunity automatically means saying no to someone or something else. And this virtually ensures you'll miss what's really important for you.

One of the costs we men often fail to calculate is the cost of our dream on our family. When you think God is calling you to do something that will require you to say no to the legitimate emotional, physical, and spiritual needs of your family, think again. It might be the right opportunity, but it is probably the wrong time.

Living as a Faithful Steward

1. Read James 2:14-17 again. How do you balance this passage with what you've learned in this chapter?

2. If you are considering a new opportunity (or evaluating a current activity) has the material in this chapter helped you reach any conclusion about how you should proceed?

3. Read Romans 12:3-8 again. How important is it to do the work for which God designed you?

4. How concerned is your boss about your job fit?

5. How does your current work, volunteer job at church, and role at home fit who God designed you to be?

6. How can you go about making adjustments for a better fit?

7. When have you been tempted to run ahead of God?

8. What open doors would you like others to be praying with you for?

9. What can you do to take one step closer to what God is putting on your heart to do?

PART THREE
LEADING YOUR FAMILY

By all means marry. If you get a good wife you will become happy, and if you get a bad one you will become a philosopher.
SOCRATES

The value of marriage is not that adults produce children, but that children produce adults.
PETER DE VRIES, American editor and novelist

One night a father overheard his son pray: *Dear God, make me the kind of man my daddy is.* Later that night, the father prayed, *Dear God, make me the kind of man my son wants me to be.*
UNKNOWN

Why Women Need Men (and Vice Versa)

The curse which lies upon marriage is that too often the individuals are joined in their weakness rather than in their strength—each asking from the other instead of finding pleasure in giving.   SIMONE DE BEAUVOIR, *French novelist and essayist*

The bridal industry is a fifty-billion-dollar-a-year business. Women still dream of walking down the aisle and marrying Prince Charming in a fairy-tale wedding—and spend a lot of money making it happen. But nowadays they are waiting longer to tie the knot. The average age women marry is now twenty-five. That's a significant change from just fifty years ago, when it wasn't unusual for a woman to marry right after high school. A hundred years ago, it was very difficult for a woman even to survive without a man. But today she has options.

In some ways, women's newfound freedom reflects healthy changes. We've not always been fair to women. It hasn't been too many years since physicians, attorneys, and politicians were expected, except on rare occasion, to be men, and if you saw a reckless driver, you automatically assumed a woman was behind the wheel. But what started as a quest to level the playing field has gotten out of hand in some ways in the past thirty years.

Peruse the Internet for a few minutes, and you can find posts from thousands of disgruntled feminists and women burning with resentment toward men. Romance novelist Carol Ann Culbert Johnson, who categorized males into twenty-three subspecies, summarized her findings and feelings like this: "In reality, who needs men because they have more problems than a mental patient. I just don't need the stress or the headaches. I['d] rather be alone, and then some. It's the best policy for me, and I'm sure most women will agree. Do you really want the headache?"[1]

And now, with sperm banks and in-vitro fertilization . . . well, the women who would rather not deal with us don't really have to.

Although it's painful to confess, from day one men have added plenty of fuel to the fire. Just look at how Adam blamed Eve when God confronted him with his failure to act responsibly. After eons of untrustworthy behavior, why should we expect women to have faith in us? But despite our bad behavior, women, though they may complain, still want us. And though they may not want to admit it, they need us—just as we need them. This isn't because we are psychologically weak, but because God made us this way. Genesis 2 states that woman completed man, so clearly male and female are incomplete without each other. Men need families and families need men—no matter what feminists may argue. Studies show that women and children are not better off without us; men make unique contributions to their families, which we will see in this chapter and the ones to follow. Marriage and family are God's ideas. (It's this learning to live together that's the rub.)

Peaceful Coexistence

Whether you are single or married, you can embrace your God-given responsibility to respect, honor, and protect the women in your life, including your mom, your sister, and your female co-workers and friends. Yet most men will marry, and the Bible invests a lot of time describing the additional responsibilities of married men.

Scripture includes numerous accounts of men *and* women behaving badly. Adultery, divorce, murder, jealousy, betrayal, they're all there. But it also describes the kind of relationship between a man and a woman that God intended—a revolutionary relationship far different than can be found in either traditional or modern societies throughout history. In fact, we find clear, specific instructions the Master gave men about our responsibility as stewards of our marital relationship.

But before we look at a man's leadership responsibility in marriage, I want to make something clear. Marriage is a two-person proposition; it takes two people to create a good marriage. I've spent countless hours with men and women who wanted to know what they could do to heal their marriage and make it a loving, fulfilling experience. There are certainly things each person can contribute to those goals, but there is nothing one person can do that will guarantee a happy marriage. It's never one person's choice. However, one person can make a huge difference—for better or for worse.

> *Some of us are becoming the men we wanted to marry.*
> GLORIA STEINEM

Even though you cannot control your wife's attitudes and actions, you make it incalculably easier for her to respond positively to your leadership when you act as the responsible steward of the relationship. But there are no guarantees that what you do will win the heart of your wife. This is not something you control. Also, regardless of whether your wife responds positively to you or whether you feel like it, you are still responsible before God to treat her with love. We are accountable before God to be a covenant partner, a romantic lover, and a sacrificial leader to our wives. Let's look at each of these responsibilities.

A Covenant Partner

It is certainly not evident based on the divorce rate among Christians, but most married couples stand before a pastor or another licensed official and make a verbal covenant with each other. Although the no-fault divorce law has made marriage vows seem like a "play" contract, God doesn't see it that way. He is serious about the promises we make before Him, and marriage is no exception. As men, we must pay attention to a number of characteristics of this covenant of marriage.

1. **Marriage is unconditional.** I've performed a lot of marriage ceremonies in my day and attended countless more weddings, but there's one vow I have never heard repeated: I've never heard a couple make a conditional "if-then" statement, such as *If you love me, then I will respect you* or *If you treat me right, then I will treat you right* or *If you bring me flowers, then I'll give you sex.* Take a look at the traditional wedding vow.

> I, _____, take you, _____, to be my wife/husband, to have and to hold, from this day forward, for better, for worse; for richer, for poorer; in sickness and in health; to love and to cherish, till death do us part, and thereto I pledge you my faith.

I've often wondered what these words mean to some couples. Perhaps the following is more true than some would want to admit.

To have and to hold, from this day forward
Groom: I get sex whenever I want it.
Bride: Finally, someone who will love me for who I am, forever.

For better, for worse
Groom: Things are good right now. What could go wrong?
Bride: Nothing could ever tear us apart.

For richer, for poorer
Groom: Finally, I found a woman who cares more about love than money.
Bride: It won't take too long for him to make as much as Daddy.

In sickness and in health
Groom: I'll have someone to care for me like Mom did when I'm sick.
Bride: He'll have compassion and comfort me when I have PMS.

To love and to cherish, till death do us part
   Groom: I get sex whenever I want it.
   Bride: Finally, someone who will love me for who I am,
      forever.

Okay, I admit I'm exaggerating to make a point. But I think it's good for us all to be jolted a little every once in a while, even in jest, and to remember the seriousness of the vows we made. Note two things about the traditional vow. It is the promise of future love—not present—and it is love regardless of future circumstances. Marriage is a unilateral commitment on your part to the welfare of the woman you married. (That means you keep your end of the agreement even when you think she isn't living up to hers.) That's serious, and even if we didn't understand that when we married, well, our obligations before God exist whether we like it or not. I suspect that there's not a man or woman alive who hasn't thought at some point in marriage, *This is not what I had in mind.* No one gets what they expected. There is simply no way to know what the future will hold or how you or your mate will respond. But despite the ebb and flow of feelings and the inevitable ups and downs of life, marriage is a solemn promise of consistent commitment.

> *Love is an ideal thing, marriage a real thing; a confusion of the real with the ideal never goes unpunished.*
> GOETHE

2. **Marriage is permanent.** The biblical covenant of marriage has no exit clauses. In a day when women were dependent on men for protection and provision, it's obvious why this was so important. But the Bible never argues for permanence based on physical expedience. Instead it offers a spiritual reason: "For this reason a man will leave his father and mother and be united to his wife, and they will become one flesh" (Genesis 2:24).

In some way beyond our understanding, the two become one in God's eyes. Though Jesus said Moses permitted divorce "because your hearts were hard" (Matthew 19:8), it is clear that this is not God's intention. Scholars debate the details, but the Bible is adamant that one partner can't just arbitrarily decide to end the marriage. Divorce is an option only if one partner breaks the covenant by certain actions—immorality, adultery, or desertion. Even then, divorce isn't automatically required, and gracious forgiveness of the offending party is encouraged.

But there's another reason for permanence. The marriage relationship teaches us about God's love for us. It schools us in what it means to forgive, what it means to serve and to give ourselves without reserve to another. I like the way my friend Dr. Mark Woods sums it up. He says that marriage is the institution that keeps us together until we learn to love each other. That pretty much says it all. It's sad that many men choose to drop the course.

3. **Marriage is exclusive.** The covenant between man and woman in marriage creates restricted air space. It is a "no fly" zone for anyone else, including parents, children, friends—anyone. Besides your relationship with God, no person or thing is to have more importance in your life than your wife. A mistress isn't necessarily another woman; it can be our work, a sport, a hobby, TV—fill in the blank. It wouldn't hurt to take a personal fidelity check regularly by asking ourselves some direct questions: Have we said *no* to our wife lately in order to say *yes* to something or someone else? Does our checkbook, calendar, or phone log reflect that another commitment is more important than she is? Do we find anything or anyone occupying space in our schedules or minds that belongs to her?

4. **Marriage is an equal partnership.** In the ancient Near East, women had very little status, and yet the marriage covenant was a relationship between equals in God's eyes. Though written at a time when many men considered women as little more than property, the Bible portrays marriage as a relationship between friends. Proverbs describes an adulteress as a woman who has

"left the partner of her youth" and ignored the covenant she made before God (Proverbs 2:16-17). The Hebrew word translated *partner* here implies an intimate friend. She is not an inferior, and she is not a rival. She is an equal.

Friends walk side by side. They share a common destination. They hold each other up when the other slips or falls. They confront each other's weaknesses. They sharpen each other's resolve. They work together. Though Ecclesiastes 4 does not refer directly to marriage, perhaps this need for friendship is why this passage has become so popular in wedding ceremonies.

> *Two are better than one, because they have a good return for their work: If one falls down, his friend can help him up. But pity the man who falls and has no one to help him up! Also, if two lie down together, they will keep warm. But how can one keep warm alone? Though one may be overpowered, two can defend themselves. A cord of three strands is not quickly broken.* Ecclesiastes 4:9-12

A Romantic Lover

It's hard to imagine the revolutionary impact the Hebrew Bible's words on marriage would have had on people in the ancient world. Not only was a man's wife to be his friend and equal—that was revolutionary enough—but she was also to be the great *romance* of his life. Keep in mind that in traditional ancient culture, and even in some places today, marriage was about economics, procreation, and status—not personal fulfillment. Men often went elsewhere for sexual fulfillment and romantic love. But nestled in the book of Proverbs is a bit of wisdom most men are very pleased to pursue. Rather than seek sexual pleasure outside marriage, the writer says, a wise man seeks it with his wife.

> *Drink water from your own cistern, running water from your own well. Should your springs overflow in the streets, your streams of water in the public squares? Let them be yours alone, never to be shared with strangers. May your fountain be blessed, and may you rejoice in the wife of your youth. A loving doe, a graceful deer—may her breasts satisfy you always, may you*

*ever be captivated by her love. Why be captivated, my son, by
an adulteress? Why embrace the bosom of another man's wife?
For a man's ways are in full view of the LORD, and he examines
all his paths.* Proverbs 5:15-21

What starts in veiled allusion becomes graphically erotic by verse
19 and ends with a reminder that our sexuality is a stewardship responsibility. The Hebrew word translated *breast* is literally *nipple*,
and the word *captivated* literally means *intoxicated*. I am to be so
captivated by the grace and sexual pleasure that I find in my wife
and her body that my sexual appetite is satiated.

Now there's some sage advice few men will mind taking or being
held accountable for. However, it takes a lifetime to appreciate what
this means. Hebrew thinking never considered personhood separate from the body. However, today many men treat women like objects to be exploited rather than valuable individuals to be loved and
enjoyed. If you ever treat your wife like this, you can be sure you are
not looking at women like God does but as objects with anatomi-
cal amenities to be used for your gratification. Demonstrating to a
woman that you love her for who she is as a person—not because
of her shape, as beautiful as it is—takes decades of invested patience
and understanding.

I am fascinated by the idea that a man and woman in marriage
are to be both lovers and friends. In C. S. Lewis's essay on friendship he writes:

> Though you can have erotic love and friendship with the same
> person, yet in many ways there is nothing less like a friendship
> than a love affair. Lovers are normally face to face, absorbed
> in one another. Friends are side by side absorbed in some
> common interest. . . . That is why those pathetic people who
> simply want friends can never make them. The very condition
> for having friends is that you want something else besides the
> friend. If someone asks you, do you see the same truth as me,
> and the honest answer is I don't care about that, I just want
> you to be my friend, no friendship can arise. There would be

nothing for the friendship to be about. Those who are going nowhere can have no fellow travelers.[2]

Not only do we gain a fellow traveler in marriage, we gain a lover as well. And what happens when lovers become best friends? Yes, there is sexual passion, but more than that, there is passion for the destination and the contribution you see yourself making in your wife's future. Certainly there is chemistry, but what this incredible person can become is what fascinates you. You know that you can help her become that person, and you want to travel that road together. It's not just about glands; it's about her glory as well.

A Sacrificial Leader

Ephesians 5 is one of the best-known, and most debated biblical passages on marriage.

> *Submit to one another out of reverence for Christ. Wives, submit to your husbands as to the Lord. For the husband is the head of the wife as Christ is the head of the church, his body, of which he is the Savior. Now as the church submits to Christ, so also wives should submit to their husbands in everything.*
> Ephesians 5:21-24

It's likely that Paul's instructions to husbands and wives have been a bone of contention between men and women ever since he penned the controversial words. The problem, of course, is the *S* word in verse 22. "Wives, *submit* to your husbands" (emphasis mine). But interestingly, *submit* doesn't even appear in verse 22 in the Greek text. It is implied and then supplied from the previous verse: "Submit to one another out of reverence for Christ." The Greek word can mean *to place* or *rank under, to subject,* and *to obey.* As a freedom-loving American, I don't really like to be told that I have to obey anyone, so it doesn't surprise me that females liberated from arbitrary cultural limitations chafe under this passage. Dance on these hot coals all you want, but the text is very straightforward. A wife is under the headship of her husband. But my question as I read this passage is, *What is Paul's point? To get defiant divas to obey their husbands?* Not at all.

If we take verse 21 at face value, a husband is required to submit equally to his wife. But as I hope you will see, they submit in different and life-giving ways.

There's a question lurking behind these words that gives us the key to its interpretation—and it's not *Who's the boss?* In Ephesians 5, Paul discusses how Christians are to help each other experience our new life in Christ and join Him in the process of bringing to redemption all of those in our *oikos*: husbands, wives, children, grandparents, work associates, and community. Each person bears the image of God and has been designed by Him for some great purpose. Yet sin tragically disfigured His image in us, impaired our potential to reach the greatness for which He designed us, and left a painful void where He once resided inside us.

To paraphrase Ephesians 5:18, instead of trying to fill the lonely, empty spaces in your heart with things that will never satisfy, change your strategy. Turn to Christ, the source of all life and lasting satisfaction, and His Holy Spirit will fill you. As you become satiated and exhilarated in Christ, His very life will overflow from your life into serving others. This will not only bless them but you as well. And in the case of your wife, you will help her experience the holy, radiant, unblemished, and blameless person she is in Christ.

I realize it may jolt some men to learn that Ephesians 5 is not a license to remind their wives of a man's head-of-the-home status, which some men tragically do for their own selfish benefit. The context of Ephesians 5 is family *ministry*, not family government. Paul is answering the question: *How do I help my mate experience what Christ has done for him or her?* Read the entire passage about marriage with that question in mind.

> *Submit to one another out of reverence for Christ. Wives, submit to your husbands as to the Lord. For the husband is the head of the wife as Christ is the head of the church, his body, of which he is the Savior. Now as the church submits to Christ, so also wives should submit to their husbands in everything. Husbands, love your wives, just as Christ loved the church and gave himself up for her to make her holy, cleansing her by the washing with*

water through the word, and to present her to himself as a
radiant church, without stain or wrinkle or any other blemish,
but holy and blameless. In this same way, husbands ought to
love their wives as their own bodies. He who loves his wife loves
himself. After all, no one ever hated his own body, but he feeds
and cares for it, just as Christ does the church—for we are
members of his body. "For this reason a man will leave his father
and mother and be united to his wife, and the two will become
one flesh." This is a profound mystery—but I am talking about
Christ and the church. However, each one of you also must love
his wife as he loves himself, and the wife must respect her
husband. Ephesians 5:21-33

Looking at this passage from the vantage point of *mutual* submission makes all the difference in the world—especially in your marriage. First, how does a woman fulfill her role in the redemptive process and help her husband discover the greatness God put in him? By treating him with the respect and honor due an intimate partner and coworker in God's kingdom. She also is willing to submit to her husband's headship as she should to Christ Himself.

Let me ask the question in a different way to help clarify what Paul is getting at here. What is the most convincing evidence that a person is gifted as a leader? It is not the acclaim or praise of people, or even the leader's own personal confidence. It is other people's willingness to follow. But understand that people's willingness to follow does not *make* a person a leader. It does, however, confirm his standing as a leader and build his confidence. It powerfully communicates, *You are a leader!* When our wives show a willingness to come under our headship, it does not make us a leader—or even trustworthy to lead. Only Christ is capable of doing that. But it does serve as a graphic reminder of the man God created and re-created us to be. A woman submits and surrenders her deepest longing for security to our deepest longing for significance by speaking to our greatest fear as a man—that we are not enough—and inspires our faith with the divine empowerment that is ours as a redeemed man. But as much as a wife's responsibilities to her husband fascinate me as a man, the practical question you and I must ask ourselves daily is: *How do I help my wife discover the greatness and stunning beauty God put in her?*

We will consider ways to build up our wives in the next chapter, but let's not move on without pausing to meditate on the remarkable responsibility and great honor God has given to you and me—guys who regularly blow it and wonder why we're not on God's List of Last Resort when He's looking for men to carry out His redemptive Kingdom work. Amazing, isn't it? No matter what you've done and no matter how you presently see yourself, you can decide right now to believe the truth of who God says you are: an empowered steward-leader, capable of giving yourself away sacrificially in service to your wife and others whom God loves and has entrusted to your care.

In Christ there is hope to rise above our wives', the world's, or even our own personal assessment of our inadequacy as men. That's why Paul prays in Ephesians:

> *For this reason I kneel before the Father, from whom his whole family in heaven and on earth derives its name. I pray that out of his glorious riches he may strengthen you with power through his Spirit in your inner being, so that Christ may dwell in your hearts through faith. And I pray that you, being rooted and established in love, may have power, together with all the saints, to grasp how wide and long and high and deep is the love of Christ, and to know this love that surpasses knowledge—that you may be filled to the measure of all the fullness of God. Now to him who is able to do immeasurably more than all we ask or imagine, according to his power that is at work within us.*
> Ephesians 3:14-20

There's power at work within us! Now there's some food for a man's soul that no one can take away from us. Do you believe that? If you can imagine being the man and husband God created you to be, you are capable of becoming that person by God's power.

Living as a Faithful Steward

Sure, it's hard to grasp the truth of who we are in Christ when the world has trained us to believe we are inadequate. That's why Paul makes this a matter of serious prayer—and so should we. Taking time to consider the following questions will also help you consider your role in your wife's life.

1. When you last saw the woman you love, did you remind her of her acceptance and security in Christ? If so, how? If not, how could you do so in the future?

2. Where do you feel most competent as a man when it comes to a relationship with a woman?

3. Where do you feel most inadequate?

4. What is the biggest barrier standing in the way of your loving a woman as the Bible describes?

5. Read the following verses and discuss what they mean to you as a man attempting to love a woman as God would have you love her.

   Romans 8:38-39
   1 Corinthians 10:13
   Philippians 4:13
   Colossians 2:9-10
   1 John 1:9

6. What is one thing you can do today to express love to the woman in your life?

Bringing Out a Woman's Beauty

He is half of a blessed man. Left to be finished by such as she; and she a fair divided excellence, whose fullness of perfection lies in him.   WILLIAM SHAKESPEARE, *King John*

Beauty is big business. In 2006, Americans spent about $14 billion on cosmetic procedures, $3 billion on makeup, and $2 billion on skin care.[1] I wouldn't be surprised to learn that a significant portion of that money was spent in Dallas. At least since the late 1960s, when I was a student at Southern Methodist University, Dallas has had a reputation for having more than its share of beautiful women. Over a hundred spas, aestheticians, and nail salons operate within a seven-mile radius of my home in north Dallas.

Don't get me wrong. I think it's a good thing that women want to look their very best and enhance their God-given beauty. But there's not enough skin cream, Botox, and plastic surgeons in the world to make a woman truly know that she is beautiful and she is loved. Only Christ can do that, but a man can remind his wife of who she is in Christ and the beautiful creature He is re-creating her to be. According to Ephesians 5, this is one of the most important parts of our role as a steward-leader, and in order to fulfill this leadership responsibility toward our wives, three significant changes must take place in our lives. Before we consider these three changes, let's review Paul's instructions to men.

Submit to one another out of reverence for Christ. . . . Husbands,
love your wives, just as Christ loved the church and gave himself
up for her to make her holy, cleansing her by the washing with
water through the word, and to present her to himself as a
radiant church, without stain or wrinkle or any other blemish,
but holy and blameless. In this same way, husbands ought to
love their wives as their own bodies. He who loves his wife loves
himself. After all, no one ever hated his own body, but he feeds
and cares for it, just as Christ does the church—for we are
members of his body. "For this reason a man will leave his father
and mother and be united to his wife, and the two will become
one flesh." This is a profound mystery—but I am talking about
Christ and the church. However, each one of you also must love
his wife as he loves himself, and the wife must respect her
husband. Ephesians 5:21, 25-33

How do we do this? Quite simple, we need a change of agenda, a change of purpose, and a change of focus.

1. **A steward-leader loves his wife sacrificially.** Being a steward-leader of your wife means changing your agenda from your welfare to her welfare. Paul's words in Ephesians 5 are packed with powerful images that describe a husband's submission to his wife. He says that as a husband I am to love my wife "just as Christ loved the church and gave himself up for her." The Greek verb *paradidomi*, translated "gave up for" has two prominent meanings: *to hand over* or *deliver up* (in judgment or as a sacrifice) and *to betray*. Paul uses Jesus' self-sacrifice as the model for our love for our wives, but the other meaning applies as well. In one sense Jesus betrayed His own self-interest for ours. Jesus didn't hold on to His own glory and position, or the wealth and status of heaven. Paul describes this model of the submissive leader in his letter to the Philippians.

   Your attitude should be the same as that of Christ Jesus:
   Who, being in very nature God, did not consider equality
   with God something to be grasped, but made himself nothing,
   taking the very nature of a servant, being made in human
   likeness. And being found in appearance as a man, he humbled

himself and became obedient to death—even death on a cross!
Philippians 2:5-8

As a woman submits to her husband by sacrificing her need to protect herself, God calls men to submit by sacrificing their own personal life in preference to their wife's welfare. This is what love does. But Paul is suggesting much more than giving my physical life in exchange for my wife's safety. It changes my allegiance, my deepest commitment, from my personal agenda to her welfare. Of the four Greek words for love, the one Paul uses here, *agape*, means *to act* for the ultimate good of the one loved. It is industrial-strength, unwavering commitment. When the well-being of our wives is at stake, nothing gets in the way. Not our convenience. Not our work. Not our pride. Not our comfort. Not our dreams.

When Kathy began writing professionally, I had to make some serious adjustments. At first I encouraged her efforts. She felt energized and was doing something that she loved—and we enjoyed the extra income. But soon reality hit: We were now a dual-career family. One day I woke up to the fact that she expected me to do more of the housework, cooking, and child care than I'd been used to. I had to limit my dreams and goals to accommodate her calling to influence women. I realized this wasn't just about me anymore. Then when the phone began to ring more for her than for me, I had to watch my ego. Now twenty years later, I realize that our marriage, our boys, and I have all been enriched because I adjusted my agenda and attitude to accommodate what we both believe God has called her to do.

C. S. Lewis defines agape love as "a state not of the feelings but of the will; that state of the will which we have naturally about ourselves, and must learn to have for other people."[2] Paul's command for a man to love his wife as his own body is exactly the point. Note that we may not particularly like our body—its shape, the pain it produces, or another physical condition we must endure—yet loving it means we desire its welfare. We feed it, care for it, and give it what it needs to sustain life and ward off illness. We give it what it needs to flourish. In the same way, there are times when a man may not like his wife. He may have noticed some legitimate flaw in her character or behavior that is selfish, unpleasant, or irritating. Or he may dislike her because he wants something from her that she will not or cannot give. Regardless of our feelings, though, we still are instructed to seek her welfare spiritually, physically, emotionally, and socially—not always an easy assignment.

When we are battling negative feelings, the only way to seek our wives' welfare above our own is to choose to have a Christlike perspective that is empowered by His supernatural love. Trying to love someone who is not always lovable in our own strength is tantamount to trying to swim from California to Hawaii. All the self-discipline and positive thinking you can muster won't get you very far. Only as we submit to Christ and His authority in our own lives can His Holy Spirit fill us with the strength to love our wives in their unloveliest moments.

> *A great marriage is not when the "perfect couple" comes together. It is when an imperfect couple learns to enjoy their differences.*
> DAVE MEURER

Here's how this happens. As Christ begins to work in my life, I am able to look at my wife in a new way—not diminishing her faults, but seeing her as Jesus now sees her, her sins forgiven and the spiritual beauty she is becoming by His grace. As the spectrum of His light falls upon her, I begin to see what He made her to be and is now re-creating her to become. To paraphrase C. S. Lewis, if we really got a glimpse of what God will ultimately do in our wives, we would likely be tempted to fall down and worship them.

My mind, aware of her true identity from God's Word, begins to rule my will, empowering and overriding my emotions, and enabling me to choose to act in a loving way. According to Lewis, something not out of the realm of the miraculous happens to us when we love like this: We find that feelings begin to follow our behavior. "When you are behaving as if you loved someone, you will presently come to love him. If you injure someone you dislike, you will find yourself disliking him more. If you do him a good turn, you will find yourself disliking him less."[3] The more I correct my vision by seeing my wife through God's eyes and treating her accordingly, the more feelings of love I will experience toward her.

In chapter 4 I mentioned the unwelcome news my wife and I received at the beginning of 2007. Eight days into the new year we learned that Kathy had breast cancer. That was the first of a number of surprises—some good, some not so good. One of my surprises, however, was how Kathy saw herself postmastectomy and reconstruction when she looked in the mirror. I thought the surgeon was an artist, but she saw scars. My physician friend Walt Larimore reminded me how emotionally traumatic the experience of losing a breast and getting used to a new one really is to a woman. Forget the fact that we had gotten through a life-threatening disease, the first few months after surgery Kathy saw herself as damaged. Walt suggested that when I caught her looking into the mirror I should take her face in my hands, look her in the eye, and tell her, "I'm your only mirror—and I think you are beautiful." That was my assignment: to help her see herself as she truly is, a physically beautiful woman who incidentally has some minor scars. As I thought about this, I realized this is exactly what God asks us to do for our wives spiritually in Ephesians 5.

How we feel about ourselves at the moment has a lot to do with how we respond to and what we mirror back to our mates. This means that the times when my wife is acting the ugliest are the times she most needs me to be her mirror reminding her how beautiful and valued and loved she is—despite the fact that she is acting less than lovely at the moment. In order to do this, I've got to make sure I'm drawing on my identity in Christ to reflect His love to her.

2. A steward-leader helps his wife change for her sake and God's glory. As I've worked with hundreds of couples over

the years, I've discovered that generally a woman will stand
at the altar with undaunted optimism that she can change the
man she is marrying into who she wants him to be. A man,
on the other hand, marries the woman he wants; then when
she doesn't live up to that image he thought he was marrying, he wants to change her back into the person he thought
he had married. This is a recipe for relational disaster. Every
one of us has an inherent selfish streak that we've polished and
perfected through many years of practice. Most of us bring this
egocentricity into marriage. The desire for someone to meet our
needs runs deep in every person. And it is probable, whether or not we consciously recognized it, that we were attracted
to our mate initially by the thought, *This is the one who will
complete me, do what I want to do, see things my way, and meet
all my needs for love, affection, companionship, significance, and
security.*

But it doesn't take long for reality to hit. You wake up in
the morning and think to yourself, *Who is this woman?* Interestingly, Paul doesn't contradict our notion that our wives need
to change. God agrees. Women are full of deficiencies, faults,
and failures. They can be critical, judgmental, manipulative,
and sometimes downright mean. Just the fact that Jesus is going
about the business of making His bride clean—spotless, stain-
less, without blemish—indicates that there may be more beast
in the beauty than you originally saw. Think about the words
the Bible uses to describe us—the bride of Christ—before the
wedding: ungodly, vile, an enemy, hostile, disrespectful, and
rebellious, just to name a few. You are not wrong to hope for
change if you see qualities such as these in the woman you
married. Paul doesn't suggest you reconsider your desire to
see your wife change but rather your purpose for wanting her
to do so.

The changes your wife needs to make might have little or
nothing to do with what you need or want. Rather she needs to
be transformed into the person God intended her to be—which

will actually benefit you as well. The terms Paul uses to describe what Christ is doing to His bride—making her "radiant," "without stain or wrinkle or any other blemish"—suggest beauty, health, symmetry, and godly character. If you are to follow Christ's example, you need to adjust your aim to align with God's goal and ask yourself: *What am I doing to help my wife grow into what Christ has made her to be?* Our responsibility to help our wives find and pursue what God wants them to *be* sometimes requires us to respond positively and other times negatively to their attitudes and behavior.

Let's look at the positive first. For a man to help his wife reach her potential as the beautiful creature God intends for her to be, he needs to lead her, as well as his whole family, spiritually. I'm not just talking about leading family devotions or making sure everyone gets to church on Sunday. As the head of our home, when we lead spiritually, we set the pace, seeking out opportunities to personally grow in our relationship with Christ and seeing to it that our family members are growing as well. This is not a job a man can farm out to his wife, no matter how much easier it seems to let her do it.

Guys, if this is something you have delegated to your wife, you're in trouble. It communicates to your entire family that God is not real, or at least not important to you. If your wife and children don't see your commitment, not merely to attend church but to follow Jesus twenty-four hours a day, seven days a week, they have every right to question your love for God and for them. And as you'll see in chapter 10, a father's spiritual impact on his children is immense. The way you live your life will make a huge difference as to whether they are committed to Christ as adults or blow off God entirely.

Seeking your wife's spiritual welfare is one of your highest priorities as a man. That means becoming a student of the amazing woman God gave you so that you will know how to help her grow. Peter commands us: "You husbands likewise, live with *your wives* in an understanding way, as with a weaker vessel, since she is a woman; and grant her honor as a fellow heir of the grace of life, so that your prayers may not be hindered" (1 Peter 3:7 NASB 1977, emphasis mine).

By the way, Peter doesn't call women weaker here. He says we are to treat our wives as we treat a weaker vessel; in other words, as something of high value. Think crystal stemware versus a plastic tumbler and you'll get the picture. Take it from a veteran of thirty-six years of marriage. Women don't break easily, but they do deserve our best effort to help them grow spiritually. Even though women often seem to gravitate toward the spiritual much easier than men, they miss a perspective of God they cannot get on their own without us. This of course works both ways. Male and female tend to instinctively appreciate different aspects of God's character. Women tend to focus on God's nearness, His tenderness and love, and His nurturing nature. Men tend to focus on God's transcendence, His might, His holiness, and His glory. Separate any of these attributes from God and you've created another god—not the God of the Scriptures.

Sometimes, however, helping a woman become more like Christ requires us to be loving as well as firm, resistant, and confrontational about her poor behavior or attitudes. When the Bible talks about the submission Christians should have toward one another, it does not mean we are to put up with rudeness or abuse. The Bible nowhere defines love as having so little self-regard that you allow yourself to be ill-treated. Biblical submission is not about rolling over and playing dead under mistreatment, whether it's physical, mental, or emotional.

If I am my wife's friend and her partner, and love her as Christ loves me, I will love her too much to sit passively by when her behavior is destructive. The most unloving thing you can do for a selfish woman is to give her what she wants or remain passive when she seeks to gain security by controlling her circumstances. If a man loves his wife, he must be willing to inflict a loving "wound" by graciously and firmly confronting the wrong. Proverbs reminds us: "Wounds from a friend can be trusted, but an enemy multiplies kisses" (Proverbs 27:6).

3. **A steward-leader avoids using his wife as his source of significance.** At times it's not all that hard to find things about my wife—some legitimate, some selfish—that I think she should change. I've confronted Kathy about some of these things—sometimes in the wrong way. More times than I care to admit, my confrontational words have been driven more by my own poor self-image than my desire for her spiritual growth. These two motivations—to meet my own needs for significance and to help her become Christlike—will always be tangled here on earth. Although our old nature, inadequate as it was, has been crucified, it still whispers from the grave. It's as if I live with a bad dog and a good dog in my head. The good dog is saying, *She's under a lot of stress right now, so she's saying things she doesn't really mean. This is not who she really is, and not who she wants to be. You need to gently remind her of who she is in Christ—a godly wife, and a kind and patient woman who seeks to reflect God's image in her words and actions.*

Then the bad dog bears his teeth and snarls in my ear: *She is so selfish. She doesn't care about you. She's living in her own world. She doesn't really love you. Why should you love her?* Can you relate to this dog fight? If you listen to the bad dog, you'll focus on what you want—and it

> *God can't give happiness apart from himself, because it is not there.*
> C. S. LEWIS

won't be pleasant for anyone. Remember, though, that in Christ, the bad dog has been caged and muzzled. It only has power when you feed it and let it loose. The more you feed the bad dog scraps of resentment and dangle replays before his eyes, the more he'll fight to be uncaged.

It's not a coincidence that the height of my selfishness as a husband came at the height of Kathy's selfishness as a wife. It doesn't really matter who took the first step down the road that led us to live in two separate worlds. No action or attitude on Kathy's part justified my attitude toward her. When things are amiss in our relationship, as the steward-leader of my family, the buck stops here.

In the mid-1990s, we were both enjoying a season of success in our careers. We were both writing books and in demand as speakers. We were living in the same house, but emotionally there was a huge gulf between us. I grew increasingly angry and frustrated over Kathy's independence. She seemed oblivious to my needs because her work had become her priority. Funny how the fact that I felt neglected mattered more to me than the misplaced priority I put on my own work, which was causing me to neglect her. Her selfishness fed my self-righteousness. At the low point in this downward spiral, Kathy chose to pursue a business opportunity that I knew was wrong. Choosing not to seek my advice and pray together over the matter, she plowed ahead. After all, she was a savvy businesswoman and I was just her naive pastor husband.

So what did I do? Probably the most unloving thing I have ever done to her. I went passive. Knowing how determined she was to pursue this opportunity, I did not confront her. Instead, I repressed my resentment over her independent attitude and chose to sit back to see what would happen. Predictably, it turned out to be a disaster. Had I known the personal pain I'd experience from the fallout, I would have been all over Kathy from the start, driven by my own selfish self-interests. However, what grieves me most now is the pain I needlessly caused her by failing to be the leader God called me to be: to love her enough to confront her willfulness, even though I would have taken some heat. I regret that I did not seek her welfare above my own pride, stepping between her and what I knew to be a bad decision and reminding her of who she was in Christ. I just wasn't man enough to do it.

Kathy and I will celebrate our thirty-seventh anniversary this year—by the grace of God. We'll both admit that we've been happily married for only about twenty-nine years. Today, ten years since my greatest failure as a husband, we're still paying for my passivity as a man, but we love each other more than ever.

When I was tempted to demand that Kathy make me feel significant, I reminded myself of my spiritual identity. I reviewed passages like these daily, reminding myself of the reality of how God saw me.

> *Therefore, if anyone is in Christ, he is a new creation; the old has gone, the new has come!* 2 Corinthians 5:17

> *I have been crucified with Christ and I no longer live, but Christ lives in me. The life I live in the body, I live by faith in the Son of God, who loved me and gave himself for me.* Galatians 2:20

> *I can do everything through him who gives me strength.* Philippians 4:13

In Christ, I am as significant and adequate as I ever desired to be—and more. At the same time, I am capable of acting more wickedly than I can possibly imagine. But I am more loved, accepted, and powerful than I ever dreamed. If this is how God sees me now in Christ, what selfish, twisted version of reality can cause me to demand my wife or any other human being to make me feel good about myself?

Living as a Faithful Steward

You and I have been charged with an incredible mission in marriage: to bring out the internal beauty of the woman God gave us. And, if you ask me, this is the most dangerous job in the universe. It requires that we present ourselves before these powerful female creatures weaponless, armorless, and selfless. Whoever called females the weaker sex was either brainless or had never made himself vulnerable with one of these awesome creatures. We may be able to out-arm-wrestle our wives, but we're no match for their emotional firepower. They are formidable creatures by design and by long training in protecting themselves from untrustworthy men. So gird up your loins, arm yourself with Christ's love and adequacy, and enter your lioness's den. You may get scratched—sometimes even severely—but she cannot deal the deathblow to the new man you are in Christ. Remind yourself of who you are and step into the responsibility Christ has charged you with: to help your wife become the holy and radiant beauty she is in Christ.

1. Evaluate your passivity factor at home. Rate yourself between 1 and 10, one being totally passive, ten being totally engaged.

2. What has passivity cost you in the long run?

3. What will it cost you to reengage as a leader?

4. In most of your interactions with your wife, does she bring out your feelings of inadequacy, or does she express confidence in your leadership?

5. How do you want to change? Discuss how you answered the questions above and what you plan to do about it.

6. If you're studying this book in a group, how could you help each other become better steward-leaders to your wives? Ask for help and accountability.

CHAPTER 9

The Wind beneath Her Wings

When a wife has a good husband it is easily seen in her face.
GOETHE

In 1993, like many other Americans that year, I read James Waller's best-selling book *The Bridges of Madison County*. It wasn't so much the deceit and adultery of Francesca, the lonely Italian Iowa house-wife, that jolted me—though that was bad enough. What hit me like a two-by-four was the ease with which men can totally ignore the dreams of their wives. Francesca and her GI husband had returned from Italy and World War II to his Iowa farm, where she dutifully raised their children. She went through the motions of life and sup-pressed her dreams, which were dismissed by her husband. When a *National Geographic* journalist showed up to photograph the pictur-esque covered bridges in Madison County, she was an easy target for a man of the world who was living a life of adventure.

Don't get me wrong. I'm not in any way condoning Francesca's choice. But sometimes such stories serve to remind us of important truths. In this case I was struck by the fact that if a man ignores the dreams and aspirations of his wife, he is setting her up for a stifled, unsatisfying life, which makes her vulnerable not only to sin, but to poor physical and mental health as well.

Men (myself included) have the unfortunate tendency to worry more about what's for dinner, if our clothes are clean, and if we can get a good tee time than about helping our wives discover what God has put in their hearts to do. From God's perspective, our wives' calling is just as important as ours, and in most cases their calling entails more than making sure the home is running smoothly so we won't be agitated at the end of a demanding day at work.

Guys, it is important that we understand our wives' giftedness and pay attention to their dreams, not only to save them from Francesca's fate, but because if we don't we could be thwarting God's purpose for their lives. There comes a time in every husband's life when he must decide whether he will be his wife's dream builder or her dream buster.

Probably none of us would stand up and shout, "You betcha . . . I want to be my wife's dream buster!" Yet sometimes it is so easy to ignore their dreams. Why is this? Well, insensitivity comes to mind pretty quickly. Would you agree that we can easily become lost in our own world and numb to the issues our wives are dealing with?

Sad but True

Diane would have been a beautiful woman at fifty, but the weight of her dilemma marred her countenance and aged her beyond her years. On the surface she had a storybook life. She lived in an expansive, beautifully appointed home, had three wonderful out-of-the-nest children, and counted important people among her friends and social connections. Her husband, Jim, was a high-profile, well-respected Christian physician. Diane had enjoyed good health until she turned forty-five, when she began to experience chronic pain and fatigue. It was then that Diane began regressing emotionally from despair to anger to depression. Her gynecologist told her it was just "that time of life," which made her angrier and more deeply depressed.

Diane experienced a lot of guilt about her physical problems and depression. After all, God had blessed her with so much. Her best friend, another physician's wife, had lost her husband to a nurse in a nasty affair and highly publicized divorce trial. Jim, on the other hand, was a rock of faithfulness, even if he could not comprehend her depression and dissatisfaction with life. Still, there was something important missing.

Over time, Diane realized she'd spent her adult life sublimating her own dreams. She had supported Jim through medical school and then raised their kids. Diane always put her family first and had no regrets about postponing her own life and dreams. Yet now that her nest was empty, she felt as if life had passed her by. She detested the thought of wasting the rest of her life like some of the other doctors' wives she knew, who filled their days with mah-jongg, shopping, and getting in on the latest gossip. But she didn't know how to quench her emptiness.

> *That is what marriage really means: helping one another to reach the full status of being persons, responsible and autonomous beings who do not run away from life.*
>
> PAUL TOURNIER

Sadly, Diane's story is not uncommon. Like Jim, many men with demanding jobs are so busy with their own lives that it never dawns on them that their wives might want something more for their lives. It's time we wake up to the responsibility to help our wives find their calling and make room for them to pursue it.

One of the ways we can be a dream buster is by holding on to the notion that one dream is enough for any family and selfishly believing that our dreams and career should take precedence over hers. Instinctively we know that if we become a dream builder to our wife, that might interfere with the fulfillment of our own dream. Heaven forbid we might have to change the way we work, alter our schedule, or modify our important plans! Quite frankly, guys, dream building really may be risky business. I know this firsthand.

I admitted in chapter 8 how my two-headed dragon—my selfish nature and my wavering sense of significance—reared its ugly head when Kathy followed her dream to write and influence women. Well, here's how this all started. About twenty years ago, I had been thinking a lot about the unique design God invested in each human being. I began to understand that a large part of my role in managing or "leading my household well" was to help my wife and boys become what God had created them to be and to help each of them find the unique role God designed him or her to play. I had no idea how to do this, so I asked God to teach me what this meant at a practical level.

After studying a number of passages on the subject, I decided to speak at a couples' retreat about some of the dream-building principles I was learning. Kathy went with me to that retreat and heard my message on Psalm 37:4—"Delight yourself in the LORD and he will give you the desires of your heart." I told the group that if our dreams are noble, right, and good, we should entertain the thought that God may have put these desires within our heart. I asked them to spend some time alone with God and write down the dreams and desires of their heart. Kathy told me she laughed as she recorded her first two dreams: 1) write a book and 2) speak to women, encouraging them to be good wives and mothers. At the next group session, Kathy didn't share her dreams with the group. Instead, she tried to push them out of her mind, thinking they were totally unrealistic. The trouble was, her dreams refused to leave her alone even when the retreat was over. They met her when she woke, chased her while she was driving, crowded her thoughts before bed, and interrupted her during spare moments in between.

Finally, when she couldn't stand it any longer, Kathy approached me with her usual Saturday honey-do list: "Fix the front door, clean out the garage, and . . . help me publish a book."

"Publish a book?" I asked.

She said she had to step out on her dream, and since I'm the one who brought up the idea in the first place, she figured I'd best help her do it. Well, as of this writing, Kathy has authored nineteen books and scores of magazine articles designed to help women manage their households. She's also spoken at hundreds of events, been interviewed on countless radio and television shows, and started a company dedicated to Family Manager coaching. It's pretty obvious: God put this dream in Kathy's heart.[1]

Today I realize that being Kathy's dream builder hasn't hurt me a bit. In fact, our lives are immensely richer for the sacrifices we have made for each other. Living with a woman who knows her calling and is happy in her work is a wonderful blessing. Plus, we have friends and an expanded mission field all over the country now through Kathy's work. Thank goodness it's one of those things I got right in our marriage. I don't take credit for Kathy's success, but I've personally witnessed how important it is for a man to encourage the dreams of his wife. All I did was help make room in our busy lives for Kathy's dream and try to remind her regularly that the incredible rush of pleasure she feels after turning in a manuscript or speaking to thousands of women is the smile of God in her heart. That's an experience I never want to hinder.

Becoming Your Wife's Dream Builder

I want to suggest some simple ways you too can lead your wife to discover her God-given calling—and earn some big points with her along the way.

1. **Jettison traditional roles and help your wife find time to dream.** Get over the idea of "men's work" and "women's work." Before you can help your wife discover her calling, you need to help her find time to think about something beyond what needs to be done around the house. Most of us guys have a minimal idea of what it takes to run a family. For example, did you know that a family of four does an average of two tons of laundry a year—and it's got to be dried, folded, and put away. (Guys, it doesn't just show up in our drawer clean and folded.) I encourage you to go to my wife Kathy's Web site, http://www. familymanager.com, and download the "Who's Responsible for What" form to see the array of tasks usually assumed by women in the home.[2] If you really want to wow her, show her the list and tell her how much you appreciate all she does. Then offer to help and to get the rest of the family on board to work together.

   Helping her carve out just thirty minutes a day to be by herself, spend time alone with God, write in her journal, and connect with the desires He has put in her heart is one of the greatest gifts you can give her. Just telling her that you want to help her do this will speak volumes of your love and commitment. But you've got to go further than just telling. You've got to do some things that some of you guys may not buy into—at least at first.

2. **Help your wife dream of what she could be.** Here's a good way to start: One night after the kids are in bed, turn off the TV and ask your wife to think about the following questions: What are the most wonderful things God could do for you, through you, with you, and in you? Listen as she expresses her thoughts. List her dreams and ideas on a piece of paper. Don't edit her remarks or make comments like "You've gotta be kidding!" Just look into the eyes of the magnificent creature over whose gift-edness God has made you a steward. Remind your beloved of her wonderful qualities. Show interest in what she's interested in. You don't have to love arranging flowers or get as excited as she does about pursuing her real estate license, but you can appreciate the fact that God made her to love those things and He might want to use those gifts to bless others. Maybe you could encourage her to take a class to hone her skill or offer to keep the kids so she could create some marketing materials to start a home-based business.

In my case, I'll readily admit that I married above my pay grade. Kathy is a competent, brilliant woman, but when we were young newlyweds her charm and physical beauty were enough to elicit the responses she wanted from people. She didn't have to reach deep inside for the abilities God had put within her. In addition, she was so accustomed to pleasing everyone else that she rarely took time to dream about what God wanted to do with her life.

Kathy was dedicated to her roles as wife and mother, but it was apparent from the start that God didn't design her to be a domestic diva. She loved to set a beautiful table, but she hated to cook. She loved the beauty of a clean, organized home but since childhood had hated to get her hands dirty. Kathy was passionate about creating the best possible atmosphere in our home, one in which our boys would develop spiritually, physically, emotionally, and socially. She tolerated a less-than-picked-up house but would not tolerate hateful words among our boys.

When I asked her to begin dreaming about what God wanted her to do with the rest of her life, I wasn't too surprised when she told me she wanted to write about families. She especially wanted to help mothers create homes where children and adults could flourish. How she'd accomplish her dream was anything but clear at first, and it would have been easy for either of us to squelch it. She had no confidence in her writing ability and wondered, *How can I write if I've never had a course in writing?* I encouraged her to pursue her dream, so she took the first step and bought some books on how to write.

3. **Start thinking in terms of "our life" . . . not your life and my life.** Kathy and I are big fans of George MacDonald, the Scottish preacher-turned-author whose writings greatly influenced C. S. Lewis. MacDonald wrote: "The highest calling of every husband and wife is to help each other do the will of God."

   Years ago this statement became the anchor of our marriage. We share it with anyone who will listen because we know the tremendous difference it makes to live together in harmony instead of fighting over whose life or calling is more important. God joined us together as husband and wife to do His will and carry forth His kingdom on planet earth. *Together* is the operative word here, and as the stewards of our households, making this idea a reality begins with us.

   I meet a lot of young couples who are headed for disaster because they begin married life with a me-mine-you-yours mentality. When a man and woman start off as competitors, guarding their territory, space, time, friendships, and bank accounts, it is impossible to grow in oneness and experience the intimacy God intended for married couples. It's as if both husbands and wives, although unbeknownst to them, are twisting George MacDonald's words using it as a self-serving maxim: You *are supposed to help* me *do the will of God,* meaning You *should take over more of the parenting responsibilities while* I *work my way up the corporate ladder,* or *My calling is more valuable than* your *calling because* I *make more money.*

> **Marriage is the highest state of friendship: If happy, it lessens our cares by dividing them, at the same time that it doubles our pleasures by mutual participation.**
>
> SAMUEL RICHARDSON

I also meet a lot of middle-aged couples who struggle with the me-mine-you-yours issue, but in a different way. They live in two different worlds—the husband engrossed in his and the wife engrossed in hers. They meet as a couple on expected common grounds—the soccer field, neighborhood barbeques, church on Sunday—but they rarely share, much less pray about, the intricate, life-impacting details of their days and their dreams for the years to come.

Their conversations revolve around bills, broken appliances, and who's going to drive the kids to which event. He dreams of retiring, getting out of the squirrel cage, and playing golf. She wonders what she's going to do when the kids leave home. She's lived for everyone else for all these years; now it's *her* time. Both of them think in terms of *me,* not *we.*

Maybe you and your wife have been living in two different worlds. You've been going through the motions of what society expects couples to do, yet your hearts have grown apart, and you're both feeling dissatisfied with life, your relationship, and what the future holds. It doesn't matter who's more to blame. It doesn't matter who's more selfish or who doesn't understand whom. What matters is that you, the steward and leader of your family, take the first step back toward the middle, start living with your wife in an understanding way, and begin helping her discover her calling. And the truth of the matter is, because God made you husband and wife, one entity to help each other do His will on earth, if God calls either of you to do something, He'll give the other of you a desire to support that dream in some way.

Living as a Faithful Steward

From personal experience, I can tell you that there is no greater joy than to see your wife pursuing her dreams, knowing you've proven to be a faithful steward. To watch an audience respond to Kathy when she's speaking before a group of women, to see her nail the script on the first take of a video shoot, to know she feels God's smile while she does her work makes me so proud and happy for her—and happy for myself for being part of making this happen.

1. How do you divide the work around your house? How do you make decisions about who does what? Is your wife happy about this arrangement? Have you asked her lately?

2. What gifts and abilities does your wife have that are going unused? How can you help her use them?

3. Are you aware of your wife's dreams and passions? What dreams do you share in common?

4. What have you done lately to help her move in the direction of her dreams?

5. What are the biggest barriers to helping your wife reach for her dreams?

6. What will it cost you to be a dream builder for your wife?

7. What will it cost you if you're not?

The Inestimable Value of a Father

One father is more than a hundred schoolmasters.
GEORGE HERBERT, *British poet*

Every father who has had the privilege of holding a minutes-old infant in his arms knows the strong desire to see his child experience happiness and a good life. After thirty-three years of fatherhood, I can tell you that this desire never goes away. The person who said that a parent is only as happy as his most unhappy child isn't far from wrong. Though my role in our boys' lives has changed as they've grown up, the desire for God's best for them is just as strong as it was when I first held them in my arms. Men who become parents through adoption or blending families also know that wanting happiness and a good life for their children is woven into the fabric of every father's being.

We wonder what our children will become when they grow up. Sometimes we get a little carried away by our dreams and think *Maybe he'll become an athlete who breaks Olympic records. Maybe she'll become a Supreme Court justice and make landmark decisions or a doctor who discovers the cure for AIDS. Perhaps he'll be a musician and have a platinum record or become CEO of a multinational corporation.*

It is good to dream grand dreams for our children, desire their happiness, but the world in which our children are growing up is affecting them in alarming ways. In response to the growing number of school shootings, researcher George Barna issued a report highlighting the critical role parents play in helping children avoid a dangerous world. He begins by painting a gloomy picture of the environment in which our children are growing up. According to Barna, the typical teenager in America absorbs almost sixty hours of media content each week— much of it violent, pornographic, or narcissistic.[1]

Barna also reports that young children feel increasingly stressed by their parents' marital and financial struggles. Many must navigate their increasingly complicated lives without the traditional safety net of an intact nuclear family, a stable group of friends, or a faith community that can convey the meaning of life and a sense of belonging to them.

According to Barna, "Most young people admit that they feel as if they do not receive sufficient attention from their parents; do not have enough good friends whom they can count on; are unsettled about their own future; have personal spiritual perspectives but not much of a sense of spiritual community; lack role models; and do not feel that they have intrinsic value."[2]

He concludes, "Parents have a huge influence on who their children grow up to become. . . . Parents cannot guarantee that their kids will behave in specific ways, but their parenting style and practices can hugely influence the likelihood of certain behaviors and perspectives."[3]

Who Needs a Father?

Male-bashing greeting cards are a dime a dozen—*If we can send a man to the moon, why can't we send all of them?* Snappy lines like this that imply the world would be better off without men may be funny to some—but not to children growing up without fathers. Nor is it funny to researcher David Blankenhorn. He argues that many of our society's worst ills are largely a result of America becoming an increasingly fatherless society. In his book *Fatherless America*, he argues that this is our most urgent social problem. He writes:

> The United States will be a nation divided into two groups, separate and unequal. The two groups will work in the same

economy, speak a common language, and remember the same national history. But they will live fundamentally divergent lives. One group will receive basic benefits—psychological, social, economic, educational, and moral—that are denied to the other group.

The primary fault line dividing the two groups will not be race, religion, class, education, or gender. It will be patrimony.[4]

The place of the father in the modern suburban family is a very small one, particularly if he plays golf.

BERTRAND RUSSELL

According to Blankenhorn, when Americans are asked, "Does every child need a father?" increasingly they are answering "No," or at least "Not necessarily." Although cultural discourse considers men superfluous or even detrimental to family life, research proves otherwise.

- Fatherless children are at a dramatically greater risk of drug and alcohol abuse.[5]
- Fatherless children are twice as likely to drop out of school.[6]
- In a study of 1,636 young men and women, researchers found that older boys and girls from female-headed households are more likely to commit criminal acts than their peers who lived with two parents.[7]
- Females between the ages of fifteen and nineteen reared in homes without fathers are significantly more likely to engage in premarital sex than adolescent females reared in homes with both a mother and a father.[8]
- Father-child interaction has been shown to promote a child's physical well-being, perceptual abilities, and competency for relatedness with others, even at a young age.[9]
- A survey of over twenty thousand parents found that when fathers are involved in their children's education, including attending school meetings and volunteering at school, children were more likely to get As, enjoy school, and

participate in extracurricular activities. They were also less likely to have repeated a grade.[10]

- In a twenty-six-year longitudinal study on 379 individuals, researchers found that fathers who spent time alone with their kids performing routine child care tasks at least two times a week raised children who became the most compassionate adults.[11]

Notice that it is not just the father's presence in the home but the quality of the father's involvement and leadership that makes the difference. George Alan Rekers writes, "Our clinical records show that in the families of disturbed boys, the mothers held the balance of power with regard to financial decisions in more than half of the families. The mothers also held the balance of power with regard to decisions concerning the children in three-fourths of these families."[12]

The sexes are not interchangeable in parenting or procreation. Rekers reports, "It is not sufficient to say merely that two parents, regardless of their sex, are better than one, because there is a unique advantage for the child in having both a female parent and a male parent. As a male, the father makes a unique contribution to the child rearing of either a son or a daughter."[13]

My own father was not so much passive as he was "absent" during the first part of my life. I loved my dad. He was a wonderful man. Everybody loved Carr Peel, but we simply weren't close. It really wasn't his fault. He didn't grow up with a father himself. How was he to know how to father? When I was fourteen, however, he showed up in spades. At the time, not only was I dealing with normal adolescent insecurity, but we had just moved to a new city and I was stressed out in a new school with more rigorous academics. On top of that I was trying to play football and play in the band too.

My day at school began with band practice at 6:30 a.m. and ended twelve hours later with wind sprints. Four weeks into the school year, I was toast. I woke up every morning with a stomachache that got my parents' attention. After a visit to the doctor—who didn't find anything wrong—I blurted out to my mom that I felt as if Dad was putting too much pressure on me. The next evening he came into my room, sat down on my bed beside me, and asked my forgiveness—and cried. Tears still well up in me as I write this over forty years later. That was the beginning of a new day in our relationship, one in which he became part of my life, spending time with me, making every one of my games even when I sat on the bench, and making me part of his world and himself part of my world. From that day on, he proved that I was a priority in his life, and it knit my heart to his. He has been dead now for twenty-seven years, and I still miss him.

The Priority

Parenting is a serious priority to God. After committing our own lives to follow Christ and serving our wives, bringing up the next generation to follow Christ is the most significant responsibility we have. As much as we would like to deflect some of the responsibility for our kids' struggles to others, we cannot blame the schools, churches, or even our culture for what's happening with children today. Sure, these entities have all failed to some degree. But the fact remains that God lays the responsibility of raising children on parents, not on schools, churches, or the government.

God has made us men the steward-leaders of our children, and if we ignore the importance of this role, we do so to our peril. You can't delegate this responsibility to the "professionals" either. Teachers, therapists, counselors, and even youth pastors are no substitute for a father's commitment. God did not prescribe a class of child-rearing experts when He instructed the new nation being formed under Moses' leadership. He placed the job of rearing kids squarely on our shoulders.

> *Love the LORD your God with all your heart and with all your soul and with all your strength. These commandments that I give you today are to be upon your hearts. Impress them on your children. Talk about them when you sit at home and when you walk along the road, when you lie down and when you get up.* Deuteronomy 6:5-7

In the New Testament, we don't find a new spiritual gift for raising children in the church. The responsibility still rests on parents, and specifically on fathers, for reasons that God clearly understood yet no researcher could prove at the time: Children need a father spiritually, emotionally, socially, and physically. A father provides inestimable value and is critical to a child's well-being. That's why when Paul writes to Timothy about requirements for church leaders, he repeats himself on this issue to make a point. In that day, Paul's readers would have understood that children were members of the household, but just so no one would miss the importance of a father's responsibility to personally lead his young children, Paul mentions them specifically. "He must be one who manages his own household well, keeping his children under control with all dignity" (1 Timothy 3:4, NASB).

Under control may be a little strong when translating Paul's Greek. The word is not as heavy-handed as it sounds to modern ears. It means *to be in a state of submission.* If we take our cues as to Paul's meaning from Ephesians 5:21 (emphasis mine), "*Submit* to one another out of reverence for Christ," leadership in the family is anything but controlling. And in one sense, a key reason children can submit to their father is because he has submitted himself to serve them.

As counterintuitive as this may sound, it works. When my boys knew I was willing to listen to their opinions and submit to their perspective or request (when I discovered that they were right on a matter), this fostered a relationship of mutual respect. When I responded to them in frustration or realized I was wrong about something, I confessed my mistake and asked for their forgiveness if I had wronged them. This didn't diminish their desire to follow my leadership; it strengthened it and opened the door for the spiritual influence I wanted to have in their lives.

Unfortunately, research indicates that the mother is more likely than the father to model spiritual practices in the home, such as saying grace at meals, encouraging Scripture memorization, and initiating bedtime prayers. She is also more likely to attend church, read the Bible, and lead family devotions[14] while dad sits passively in his easy chair—or opts out entirely. Small wonder so many children jettison church when they leave home thinking, *If Dad doesn't think it's important, why should I?*

Statistics regarding the father's spiritual influence on children are compelling. When a mother trusts Christ apart from her husband, her family follows 17 percent of the time. When Dad becomes a Christian, the rest of the family follows 93 percent of the time.[15] Accounts in the book of Acts give credence to this statistic. When the leader of the *oikos* came to Christ, the entire household followed.[16] There is a significant connection between the faith of a child and that of his father.

From my own experience, including my work with a prison ministry, I've noticed that children generally learn unconditional love from their mother. I've met a lot of prisoners with "Mom" or "Mother" tattooed on their arm—never "Dad." When I ask why they have "Mom" tattooed on their arm, these men tell me it was because they know their mom loves them no matter what they've done. As important as this kind of love is to a child, kids learn right from wrong—and the consequences—more often from their dad. If the father leaves their spiritual development to Mom, abdicating his role as spiritual leader of the family, the kids grow up confused about how life works. Without a grounding in these values, drug and alcohol abuse, sexual acting-out, and even failure in school are more likely. I believe that's why Paul addresses the male side of the parenting partnership in Ephesians and Colossians.

> *I am determined that my children shall be brought up in their father's religion, if they can find out what it is.*
>
> CHARLES LAMB

> *Fathers, do not exasperate your children; instead, bring them up in the training and instruction of the Lord.* Ephesians 6:4

> *Fathers, do not embitter your children, or they will become discouraged.* Colossians 3:21

Strategy for Failure

When I think back to the challenges of raising my children, my mind naturally goes to the frustrations *I* as a father had with my children. Interestingly, the Bible focuses on *children's* frustration with their fathers. In Ephesians and Colossians Paul addresses how Christians are to deal with all the relationships they have in their *oikos*—husbands, wives, parents, children, masters, slaves, and business associates. He begins with positive commands in all of these relationships, save one. He begins his instructions about child raising with a warning to fathers. Children's fragile, impressionable lives need special care from a father lest their frustration with us leads to discouragement, or more literally in line with the Greek, they become passionless and simply give up. Here are some actions and attitudes to avoid, as they are guaranteed to frustrate your children.

Setting a predesigned agenda for the child's life. Whether we are talking about excelling at sports, earning high grades, choosing a particular vocation, or even developing rigid patterns in one's spiritual life, forcing a child to fit a mold of your making—one that doesn't consider how God designed your child—is a sure path to frustration for both of you. It also sets up a natural conflict. As your child fails to live up to your agenda, he or she will naturally feel estranged from your love.

Trying to find your self-worth from the life of your child. Your child is not here to make you feel good about yourself. When your success in life or your success as a parent is somehow dependent upon your child's behavior or choices, selfish manipulation, in an attempt to feed your own ego, is the natural outcome.

Failing to set standards. When you fail to set limits, define unacceptable behavior, and consistently hold your children responsible for their actions, they have no idea how to act or how to please you. There is no way they can win. To fail to do this for your children speaks loudly: *I don't care!*

Setting unrealistic expectations. Be careful not to set standards that are beyond your child's ability to reach. Insisting that a child clean the kitchen "perfectly," sweep out the garage "just like I want it," or sit through a church service without wiggling may be beyond a child's ability, physically or intellectually.

Using degrading communication. Words are powerful, and despite what the old rhyme says, words can hurt you. Put-downs, sarcasm, and nagging can depress and antagonize a child.

Neglecting to spend time together. Your children want *you*, not a nanny or a day-care worker. No one can take your place. Most kids spell love T-I-M-E. Give them everything else and fail to give them your time, and your children will not know you love them.

If you are a dad who is separated from your children, you have a difficult path to follow. You may have virtually no control over the situation. But whatever you need to do to fulfill your responsibilities as a father, do it for your children's sake. Reconcile with your kids' mom, live closer to your kids, work less. Your children deserve your sacrificial best. Do whatever it takes to spend time with them.

Strategy for Success

It's both frightening and humbling to think that the way we father our children has a great influence on whether they'll become godly adults. Although we can control children when they are small, ultimately they are outside our control, so it is important to keep in mind the difference between goals and desires. My goal is to be a godly father, and I work diligently on that role. I can control that. My desire is that my children will turn into adults that trust and honor God. I cannot control that. But I can pray and provide the kind of environment that encourages them along that path. Here are some positive steps you can take to do this.

Create an atmosphere of security. It's easy to run past Paul's words "bring them up," but it's important to note that he chose words that create a descriptive image of the atmosphere our children need to prosper. The Greek word translated *bring up* literally means "to nourish," especially in the context of nursing a young child. The word portrays the tender image of a mother nursing her infant.

To gently coax a child into wanting to follow Christ, we must foster an atmosphere of security that comes from two sources: 1) the quality of the love relationship between you and your wife; and 2) the quality of the bond between you and the child.

The most loving thing a father can do for his children is to love their mother. One of the least loving things you can do as a father is to let something cause a wedge between you and your child's mother, even if it's the child. Children gain tremendous security just knowing mom and dad are committed to each other and that their relationship is the most important relationship in the house. Old notions that children are better off if unhappy parents split up has been proven to be patently false. Divorce harms children of different ages in different ways, but every man needs to realize that divorce damages children.

Maybe you are, for whatever reason, divorced or separated from your children's mother. With compassion I urge you for your children's sake, so far as it depends on you, to reconcile the relationship if at all possible. If not, make peace as much as you can with her. For your children's sake, see a counselor to learn how you can love the mother of your children as a friend, if not a spouse. And if not as a friend, learn to love her as an enemy—as the Bible commands.

Children don't care about our faith unless they know we care about them. If we want our children to love Christ, first they need to know that we love them. They simply won't value our faith if they don't know we value them. Your children need to believe you love and accept them for who they are and just as they are—not because of what they do, what they accomplish, or what they become.

Correct foolish behavior. Children enter the world as beautiful little packages of self-centered energy. Proverbs 22:15 tells us that "folly is bound up in the heart of a child." Unless someone intervenes in their lives, they will grow up to be foolish adults. The people charged with that intervention are the children's parents, and particularly, according to Ephesians 6, the father. In the context of security and unconditional love, we must discipline our children. Failure to do this is not only parental malpractice, but failure to love them as well. When a father loves his child, he corrects poor behavior. That's why Proverbs challenges sons to make sure they don't misunderstand a father's discipline: "My son, do not despise the LORD's discipline and do not resent his rebuke, because the LORD disciplines those he loves, as a father the son he delights in" (Proverbs 3:11-12).

To love means that we forgive, but it does not mean that we make excuses for bad behavior, condone bad attitudes, or put up with harmful habits. Paul says fathers are responsible to *train* our children—that is to discipline them. He picks a very common word that means "to conform to a set of behavioral standards." The goal of discipline is not just to create well-behaved children but to help them grow into self-disciplined adults. It is not intended merely to produce outward compliance but to produce an inner change of beliefs about how life works. This is what teaches children how to make wise choices.

We do this in two ways. First, we must clearly communicate to children what is acceptable and unacceptable. We do this by word and deed. Your children need to see you making wise choices—striving to model the attitudes and actions you tell them are right and refusing those you say are wrong. When your children need discipline, it's always a good idea to review your standards. If they didn't understand what they did was wrong, you have the opportunity to clarify the desired behavior and seek their agreement. If they did understand and willfully disobeyed, the review will help them clearly understand and connect their poor behavior with the consequence you are about to inflict.

Second, we must consistently follow through with consequences. We really can't control our children's behavior—not for long anyway. However, we can control the consequences of their choices. By helping your children learn that choices have consequences, you prepare them for life in the real world. Far too many young fools enter adulthood thinking that the world is here to serve them, no matter how they act. Don't be reticent to use your fatherly authority to save your children from foolish, harmful behavior. "Folly is bound up in the heart of a child, but the rod of discipline will drive it far from him" (Proverbs 22:15).

Although some take this verse to mean that corporal punishment is the universal remedy for foolishness, the Bible views discipline in a much more comprehensive way. The rod is used both literally and figuratively as an expression of authority. The point of this verse is that we must exercise our authority to create an environment of both love and appropriate consequences. Our love must be consistent and the consequences should be tailored to match the offense and the personality of the child. As you are considering the particular expression of consequence, remember the goal. It is not to hurt the child or inflict pain. It is to teach the child that his behavior has consequences so that the next time he will choose a different behavior. It is our job to thoughtfully choose the least forceful consequence that will teach this lesson. For some children all it takes is a look of displeasure, for others a firm word, for others a firm withholding of a privilege (especially if a freedom has been abused), and for others a time-out. Reserve corporal punishment for tough cases of defiance—and then only when you're sure your own anger is under control.

Never forget: Discipline is all about love, not punishment or giving children what they deserve. It's about our loving concern to teach them to reject foolishness—both by correcting bad behaviors and by teaching them right behaviors and beliefs.

Teach the truth. Paul tells us we are not only to correct; we are to teach our children the truth. Men, this is our responsibility. It cannot be delegated to the experts—pastors, Sunday school teachers, or youth workers. And don't even begin to think that you are covered if you send your children to a Christian school. If you have these *extras*—great, but if you choose to farm out the responsibility to teach your children God's truth, you're not only choosing to be disobedient, you are placing your children's lives in jeopardy.

To fulfill your responsibility you don't need to go to seminary, study the Bible ten hours a day, or do everything perfectly. You do need to take your spiritual life seriously, study God's Word for yourself, and admit your mistakes when you screw up. Over the past thirty-plus years of parenting, I've discovered that there are four components that help children learn God's ways and enter adulthood as followers of Jesus.

Incarnation. The truth we teach them must be incarnate, that is, "in the flesh." If we want children to adopt biblical values, we must hold those values ourselves and live them out consistently. Our kids need to see what it looks like to follow Jesus in our daily routines, like seeing us spend time daily with God through Bible study and prayer. They need to see us treat our wives with respect, even when we disagree. They need to watch us turn off a television program because it glamorizes sin. They need to see us reach out to help people in need.

Instruction. Kids need to know right from wrong, and we need to tell them. We wouldn't dream of letting our children drive a car without instruction. How much more important it is that they learn to steer their lives in God's direction! They can pick up a lot from our lives, but we also need to explain the rules. According to Moses, we need to be constantly aware of opportunities to teach our children the spiritual laws of life: "Talk about them when you sit at home and when you walk along the road, when you lie down and when you get up" (Deuteronomy 6:7).

I've had the humiliating experience more than once of being pulled over for speeding with a child in the car to observe the interaction. If this wasn't bad enough, a couple of the police officers were a lot more authoritarian and belligerent than necessary. I was tempted to give them a piece of my mind. Yet times like these provide natural teaching opportunities about how to stand up for yourself while still being respectful—even when authority is not being respectful to you.

Initiation. At each stage of their lives, children need plenty of opportunity to apply what they have learned personally and to receive our encouragement as they move further toward responsible adulthood. One reason so many well-taught children from good homes falter when they leave home is that they have never been given the responsibility to make their own choices and to learn the consequences of their choices.

When we do give them new responsibilities, more likely than not, they will fail at some point. When they do, we must be there to pick them up, lovingly correct them, and point them in the right direction again. Lessons learned in the pain of failure are seldom forgotten. But if a child never has the opportunity to succeed or fail on his own, he will only know the truth in theory. A gradual initiation to responsibility prepares the child to make healthy choices on his own when mom and dad are absent.

Immersion. Immersing children in a spiritual value system is really what we're doing when we consistently practice the first three principles. We let them see, hear, and experience spiritual truth in the midst of everyday living. This is what Moses was reminding the Jews of in Deuteronomy 6—that spiritual truth needs to permeate their lives 24-7.

Here's what this chapter boils down to: When it comes to parenting, God the Father is our ultimate role model. He shows us what it means to be a successful parent—and it's certainly not measured by how our children turn out. Obviously, if the perfect Parent has rebellious children, great parenting does not ensure our kids will turn out well either.

God judges our success as fathers, not by our children's behavior, but by *our* behavior. The goal of fatherhood, then, is to do our best to be a godly father. If we approach parenting that way, we will seek to serve our children rather than manipulate them to meet our own need to prove ourselves. As with every venture of stewardship, God measures us, not by outward results but by how faithfully we obey the Master's will. This gives us the freedom to love our children unconditionally.

Living as a Faithful Steward

Take time now and look over these four components of good parenting and ask yourself some tough questions. If you are studying this book in a group, discuss your answers with each other.

Incarnation

- Do my children know that I am a committed follower of Jesus?
- What decisions have I made that show my commitment to my children?
- What areas of my life need a spiritual tune-up? Are there things I would be embarrassed for my children to know?

Instruction

- How am I creatively teaching my children the truth?

Initiation

- What limitations have I put on my children? What appropriate freedoms am I extending to them?
- How can I best control consequences to teach them responsibility?

Immersion

- Do my children see what's going on in our home as different when compared to the homes of non-Christian friends?
- Do they understand that my decision-making process is based on pleasing Jesus?

Our children don't expect a perfect father, but they do expect one who loves them, admits when he fails, and asks for their forgiveness when he fails. If the Holy Spirit has convicted you of a mistake you've made with your children, it's time to come clean. Maybe you realize you haven't been the spiritual leader God expects you to be. Maybe your love has been conditional. Maybe you've been harsh and demanding. Maybe you've failed to set proper limits. It's time to make it right, take the responsibility as a steward of your children, and make the difficult choices that will lead to their welfare. No matter how hard it is, you and your children will be thankful down the road, if not now.

11

Launching Children into the World

We cannot fashion our children after our desires, we must have them and love them as God has given them to us.   GOETHE

With twenty-seven seconds left on the clock, Daniel "Rudy" Ruettiger runs onto Notre Dame Stadium's field. Not only is it the last game of his senior year, it is the first time in his college football career that he's been called into a game. As his teammates and fans cheer *"Ru-dy! Ru-dy!"* Rudy sacks the opposing team's quarterback. As a result, the game ends on the next play. Rudy is carried off the field on his teammates' shoulders, the last player in Fighting Irish history to be given that honor.

This scene is the climax of the widely acclaimed movie *Rudy*, which is based on Ruettiger's true story. One of fourteen children born to a lower class family in Joliet, Illinois, Rudy grows up dreaming of playing football at Notre Dame. But poor grades, a lack of money and talent, as well as his small physical size (5 feet 6 inches; 165 pounds) keep him working at the local steel mill with his father and brothers. When Rudy's best friend, Pete, is killed in an explosion at the mill, he decides to follow his dream of playing college football for the Fighting Irish and leaves for Notre Dame—in spite of his father's warning. In the film, his dad tells him: "Chasing your stupid dream causes nothing but you and everyone around you heartache. Notre Dame is for rich kids. Smart kids. Great athletes. It's not for us. You're a Ruettiger. There's nothing wrong with being a Ruettiger."

His dad then tries to convince him that he could make a decent future for himself at the mill, just as his brothers Frank and Johnny are doing. Rudy interrupts him and walks away, saying, "I don't want to be Frank or John."

The film's storyline illustrates an important role men play in leading their families. We have a choice to be either dream builders or dream busters. When our kids are little, it's fun to hear their ideas of what they want to be when they grow up. Often they mention wanting to design spaceships, play professional golf, or become a rock star. When they're young, we pat their heads and tell them that they are bright and talented enough to become anything they want to be. Of course, when our teenagers boast that they want to become professional skateboarders or tattoo artists, we think again about this anything-you-want-to-be platitude. And our responses to these aspirations might not be so affirming: "Are you nuts? You're going to get a real job." While Rudy persevered despite his dad's skepticism, many kids give up and distance themselves from us when we respond in that way.

There's a better way. One of your most important jobs as steward-leader of your household is to help your wife and children discover their calling and become what God created them to be. We've got to be careful and prayerful about doing this. I've met a lot of dads who have tried to mold their kids into someone or something *they* think their children should be. It's easy to fall into the trap of pushing a child toward the "right" career—one that offers prestige, pays a lot of money, provides the most security, and gives us fatherly bragging rights. When we do this, we're failing to consider our children's unique design and the dreams God has put within them.

Before Kathy and I understood this concept, we created a lot of miserable moments—for ourselves *and* our firstborn child—trying to squeeze him into a mold of our own making. For example, we dreamed of John someday playing the piano in Carnegie Hall. So we enrolled him in a preschool music program at a local university and signed him up for private piano lessons, thinking he might have some of his mother's musical genes. Many an afternoon was ruined as he tried to like this pursuit so important to his parents. The problem? John was not wired to be a musician.

But John is incredibly artistic—he has a whizlike ability on the computer and a keen entrepreneurial mind. Years ago, he sat down in front of my computer and taught himself to use the sophisticated graphics program. Does it make sense that John started a computer design business when he was in high school? Sure does. When he was in college, John came up with the idea for a graphic arts company and started it while he was still a student. Today—after a three-year sojourn in Hollywood where he picked up a lot of helpful computer and graphic art skills creating special effects for a film studio—he has grown his college business, www.StickerUniverse.com, into a thriving enterprise.

> *Parents . . . are sometimes a bit of a disappointment to their children. They don't fulfill the promise of their early years.*
> ANTHONY POWELL

Joel, our second-born son, has always loved to sell things. In kindergarten he enjoyed going door-to-door selling school fundraising products. He and his brother started a flower bulb sales business when they were in elementary school; in high school Joel loved his job at a nursery selling Christmas trees. It should come as no surprise then that today he has a booming sales and marketing business, www.HoleintheRoof.com. When Kathy and I noticed his strong aptitude in math and science, we hoped that he might pursue a career in medicine. Yet it would not have been right for us to pressure him into medical school. If he had become a physician, would he love his job today? I doubt it, unless he could figure out a way to sell products to his patients after their examinations. Starting a sales and marketing company was riskier but a lot more fun and fulfilling—and today he's enjoying great success.

At a kindergarten play, we noticed that our third son, James, loved to be behind the microphone—something that would petrify many kids. When he received his first "play" guitar that year, he informed us that he wanted to be a rock star. Now there's a comment most dads would like to write off—but if God puts the dream within the child, it will continue to come up, year after year. As I write this chapter, James has recently graduated from college with a degree in communications but has also just released his first CD at www. JamesPeelMusic.com.

Most guys I know say they don't know a whole lot about how to find direction for their own lives, much less how to help their children find direction for theirs. If that's true for you, it's nothing to hang your head about. It's a widespread problem. It amazes me that we can send people to live in space stations for months and bring them back in one piece, but we've been noticeably unsuccessful when it comes to helping people find work that really fits them. In fact, we're so inept that many students now enrolled in college are spending large sums of money preparing for careers they will leave after only a few years, and many of them will end up unfulfilled in their work no matter how many career changes they make.

One reason so many people struggle to find satisfying work is our society's belief that we can make ourselves fit into any occupation. When psychologists and sociologists debate what determines who we are, they often begin with the premise that we are shapeless when we arrive on the delivery table—like clay to be molded by the circumstances of life after we enter the world.

No wonder that when we become adults, other people think they can shape us into whatever society wants us to be, our family needs us to be, the church recruits us to be, our friends encourage us to be, our company promotes us to be, or in some instances, the government determines we should be. On top of that, we also believe the popular American "truism" that we can be anything we want to be.

Certainly external factors influence us. However, they don't explain why we are all so different—why two children raised in the same home, by the same parents, with the same privileges, turn out so completely different.

The Bible, however, is very clear on this issue. It says that, rather than a shapeless mass of human potential at birth, each one of us came with a prior design. We are not *becoming* someone—we *are* someone. Our distinct characteristics are not the result of random selection or cultural and societal influences. A purposeful God who made us in His own image designed the detailed uniqueness of every individual.

> For you created my inmost being;
> you knit me together in my mother's womb.
> I praise you because I am fearfully and wonderfully made;
> your works are wonderful,
> I know that full well.
> My frame was not hidden from you
> when I was made in the secret place.
> When I was woven together in the depths of the earth,
> your eyes saw my unformed body.
> All the days ordained for me
> were written in your book
> before one of them came to be. Psalm 139:13-16

I've often marveled that there are more than sixty billion different fingerprints currently in use. And amazingly, we can be sure that the next baby born will come with ten new, totally unique prints of his or her own. If God goes to that much trouble with our physical body, what does this say about our complex "inmost being"—the unique shape of our mind, will, emotions, and our basic strengths, abilities, and motivations? These are not "acquired" any more than blue eyes, curly hair, or long fingers. They are part of God's purposeful handiwork. We saw that earlier in Ephesians 2:10: "For we are God's workmanship, created in Christ Jesus to do good works, which God prepared in advance for us to do."

Whether we're leading a company or a family, a big part of our job is getting the right people doing the right job at the right time. Because our children come predesigned into this world, they are not ours to shape and mold according to our plans for them. We can, however, nurture or stunt their growth. This thought should make us stop in our tracks. Rather than asking who we want our children to become, we need to ask who God has made them and how can we help nurture this unique person. Inherent in Paul's directive that a church leader should "manage his own family well" (1 Timothy 3:4) is the stewardship of the individuals within the household.

Helping Your Children Discover Their Calling

Give everyone a job. It takes a family to run a family. It's a team effort, not the job of mom, or mom and dad, but everyone living under the roof. Everyone in our family worked, made a contribution, and was counted on to do their work.

As soon as they were physically able, the boys helped with housework. I remember Kathy putting a sock on Joel's hand when he was three and telling him to wipe off the baseboards. As their abilities grew, their responsibilities increased. By the time they were four or five the boys were folding laundry. And by the time they were ten they were able to do their own laundry. Of course, they didn't do things "perfectly," but as we watched them work, we began to see what they liked and didn't like to do. And interestingly, as is often the case, what one child hated to do, another one liked. Of course, there will always be jobs no one wants to do, but whenever possible we parceled out jobs based on how members were gifted. By giving each child work to do, we not only could begin to spot what they enjoyed and were good at, but we could watch their self-esteem and character grow as well. Children need to know that their family needs them, and it's also important that they learn to be a servant to others around the house.

In Romans 12, Paul points out an important principle of giftedness. A person's gifts come, not only with a stewardship, but with an authority of their own. As parents, we're in the unique position of being able to begin affirming our kids' calling by giving them dominion over some aspect of the household. At some point, each of our sons and daughters needs to know he or she has a gift that we have recognized. One way to do this with an older child is by handing over some important part of family life that relates to that gift. I'm talking about something more than delegating day-to-day responsibilities. Instead, you might entrust your child with something like creating the family's weekly dinner menus, planning your family's vacation, or maintaining your vehicles. In so doing, you not only affirm his or her value but provide an opportunity to further develop that gift.

Encourage them to dream. You, as the steward-leader of your home, are to help your children dream and consider the most wonderful things God could do for them, through them, with them, and in them.

Managing your household well also means running interference for your children when others want to squeeze them into a mold that doesn't fit. During our sons' formative years, elementary school teachers who understood preadolescent males proved to be a rare commodity. I can still see my own first-grade teacher with her hands on her hips trying to get my attention by saying, "Billy, can you tell us the answer?"

> *It is a wise father that knows his own child.*
>
> WILLIAM SHAKESPEARE,
> *The Merchant of Venice,*
> ACT 2 SCENE 2

I couldn't, of course, because once again, I'd been in a faraway world heroically saving the day in the usual way first-graders do. "Billy, you've got to pay attention."

"Yes ma'am," I always dutifully replied, resolving to do better in my childlike way. But before long I'd find myself daydreaming again about killing Martians or taming the Wild West. Much to the consternation of my parents, "Tends to daydream" appeared more than once on my report card in my early years. Eventually, I learned to practice the painful discipline of keeping my mind focused in the present. Unfortunately, I learned that lesson all too well.

Schools, teachers, and parents have a fine line to walk. Yes, it's important to teach our children how to keep on task and to help them realize that sometimes learning requires a lot of mundane grunt work. But often, kids—especially boys—daydream because school is mind-numbingly dull.

Our dreams—even daydreams—express something important about how God created us. Ever notice that kids most often dream of being superheroes, fighting villains, and winning battles? Dreams of good conquering evil are not far from what God intended for the human race. We need to encourage noble dreams in our children, not squash them, no matter how unreasonable they might sound.

Zach Hunter is an average teenage. He lives in Atlanta and just happens to be a modern-day abolitionist. He spends his summers speaking to tens of thousands of people about slavery. Zach dreams of wiping out slavery from the planet during his lifetime, whether the enslaved people are working in brick kilns, rice mills, fishing villages, or brothels. I read about Zach in an article in *Christianity Today*.

> Fifteen-year-old Zach Hunter is just like any ordinary American kid. He likes listening to music, reading, and running after what he is passionate about. By the age of 12, he had a specific passion. It was to "be the change" and abolish slavery, just as William Wilberforce did 200 years ago. Having launched the "Loose Change to Loosen Chains" programme in the seventh grade, Zach raised thousands of dollars with the intention of rescuing victims of slavery.[1]

After his mom, Penny, told him that millions of people are enslaved even today, Zach took action. His parents have been astonished to watch their introverted son enthrall huge crowds and raise large amounts of money to end this practice.

> "Knowing that he comes from a background where he struggled with anxiety and nervousness earlier in his life, and knowing that he puts himself aside, puts aside those feelings to step out, to speak out for others who don't have a voice, is truly remarkable to me and I can't believe he's my son," said his father, Gregg Hunter.[2]

In his book, Zach challenges other young men and women to dream with him. "Well, I still have those big dreams. And I believe God likes it when his kids dream big. I just turned 15 years old, and I'm a modern-day abolitionist."[3]

The first people Zach credits for inspiring him? His mom and dad. I wonder what would have happened if early on this young man's father had said, "Oh, son, I'm sorry. But there are so many hurting people in the world. There's really nothing we can do about it"?

As far as my own family goes, we're far from perfect. But I think that each member is acutely aware that it is a blessing to be part of a family that encourages each other to listen to God and dream about their purpose for their lives. That's part of our family mission—to help each other become all that we were created by God to be. As the chief steward-leader of my family's gifts, this means developing an atmosphere that encourages dreaming to become all God created each of us to be.

Be careful not to treat one child's dreams as more important than another's. For example, let's say you were an athlete in high school and you are delighted that your daughter is following in your footsteps. Your younger son has no aptitude for sports, but he's showing potential for being a good artist. Your younger daughter is happy just to putter with her dolls all day often pretending she is their teacher. It would be easy to focus on the child who shares your interests. But remember, even the younger daughter, with whom you might find it hardest to identify, has a God-given purpose. It could be that she will become a teacher, coach, or instructor of some sort—you'll find clues over time in her choices and from your prayers. Make sure you spend time playing with her, watching for clues about her design and what she likes and dislikes. Expose her to other opportunities and people, and see who and what piques her interest. In other words, become a student of your child. When you find something a younger child is interested in, look for opportunities to expose him or her to that area.

Watch your personal agenda. Before we ignore or obstruct a family member's calling, we need to be sure we're not standing in God's way. It takes parents with a strong sense of self-worth to recognize and communicate to their children that they are uniquely valuable to God and that He has a purpose for them that Mom and Dad don't determine. Be careful about taking your cues from culture—falling into the trap of pressuring your kids into the "right" things to do or be involved in— and failing to consider the unique design God put in them.

Celebrate their success. Praising, affirming, and encouraging others comes easy for some people. If these activities are easy for you, great. If not, they're still your responsibility. I know a number of grown men and women who are still trying to figure out how to please their father. Nothing they ever did was good enough. Others feel as though they never even got on their father's radar screen. As deep as a person's faith might grow, this is a debilitating burden to carry into adulthood. And the craving to receive our dads' approval never goes away if it is not met.

Someone said that you're not a man until your father tells you so. I think the same is true for women. A daughter will struggle all her life if her father fails to tell her in a way she can comprehend that she is lovely to him. The fact is, we all long for praise and affirmation. From the depths of our being, we long to hear God's praise, "Well done!" Likewise, children desperately need to know their parents are proud of them. In that sense, we stand in God's place as we praise them.

Finally, you need to be ready for the fact that, in the world's eyes, one, several, or all of your family members may become more successful than you. That possibility doesn't feel good to some men (especially if it's their wife who outshines them). Don't forget that in God's eyes we are successful when we are obedient steward-leaders. That includes helping every member of your family reach the potential for which He created them. In that way, their success is your success as well.

Be a dreamer yourself. We can help family members dream, not only when we listen and encourage their vision, but when we pursue our own God-given dreams. Dreaming is infectious. When we follow God's dreams and see those dreams become a reality, others find the courage to dream God's dreams for themselves.

One of my favorite dreamers is Nehemiah. After most of the Jews had been exiled from Israel, Nehemiah, himself eight hundred miles away from Jerusalem, dreamed something for the Jewish people in Jerusalem that they couldn't dream for themselves—to rebuild the walls of God's holy city. When he arrived there, he found the walls in worse condition than he expected, and the people who would do the work were demoralized. But when he told them what God had put in his heart to do and how "the gracious hand of my God was upon me" (Nehemiah 2:8) they replied, "Let us start rebuilding" (v. 18). And the result still amazes civil engineers and contractors to this day. Jerusalem went from ruin to habitable city in less than two months (see Nehemiah 6:15-16).

This feat was more than the fulfillment of a dream. It was more than a testimony of Nehemiah's leadership. It was even more than a demonstration of God's goodness. It resulted in the rebirth of hope for God's people. From behind those walls, they would be free to worship, free to rebuild their society, and free to dream about the future. By following his dream, Nehemiah made it possible for millions of others to dream as well. Because Jerusalem was reestablished, the Jewish nation could once again prosper. More Jews would return and resettle towns like Bethany, Nazareth, and Bethlehem. They would raise their families, knowing their children had a hope and a future. And when things were bleak, they would dream about the coming of Messiah. And when Messiah came, the drama of redemption was carried out in the shadow of those walls, making it possible for us to dream of a better world.

Living as a Faithful Steward

What about you? Would your kids consider you to be a dream builder or a dream buster? It's never too late to become a dream builder for them. Make a commitment to be a student of each of your children and honor their dreams. By giving our children work and also providing them opportunities to explore the world, we can begin to see where they "feel God's pleasure"—and equally important, where they feel no pleasure.

The following questions may stimulate your thinking as you consider ways you can be your children's dream builder.

1. What led you to the work you are currently doing? Is it something you always wanted to do? your parents wanted you to do? you just stumbled into?

2. What type of help do you wish your parents had given you? Was there any help that you wish they wouldn't have given you?

3. How serious are you about helping your children find the work God has for them? What are you doing to help them find it?

4. What differences do you see in your children already?

5. When you think of your interaction with your children, would you say you are a dream builder or a dream buster?

In nothing has the church so lost her hold on reality as in her failure to understand and respect the secular vocation. She has allowed work and religion to become separate departments, and is astonished to find that, as a result, the secular work of the world is turned to purely selfish and destructive ends, and that the greater part of the world's intelligent workers have become irreligious, or at least, uninterested in religion.

But is it so astonishing? How can anyone remain interested in a religion which seems to have no concern with nine-tenths of his life? The Church's approach to an intelligent carpenter is usually confined to exhorting him not to be drunk and disorderly in his leisure hours, and to come to church on Sundays. What the Church should be telling him is this: that the first demand that his religion makes upon him is that he should make good tables.
DOROTHY SAYERS

Wherever man may stand, whatever he may do, to whatever he may apply his hand, in agriculture, in commerce, and in industry, or his mind, in the world of art, and science, he is, in whatsoever it may be, constantly standing before the face of his God, he is employed in the service of his God, he has strictly to obey his God, and above all, he has to aim at the glory of his God.
ABRAHAM KUYPER

Your Monday Morning Mission

There is always the danger that we may just do the work for the sake of the work. This is where the respect and the love and the devotion come in—that we do it to God, to Christ, and that's why we try to do it as beautifully as possible.   MOTHER TERESA

Whether you're writing software, flying an airplane, or framing a house, your work is important to God. The God who gave us the Cultural Mandate in Genesis 1:28 ("Be fruitful and multiply," NASB) and the Great Commission in Matthew 28:19 ("Make disciples of all nations"), is the same God who is committed to meeting the legitimate needs of people and all creation. No matter where we work, God calls us to be His stewards in our workplace. As already mentioned, when Paul told Timothy to look for leaders who lead their household well, the church clearly understood that he had workplace relationships as well as family relationships in mind. In his day most businesses were in the home. In fact, workers often lived in the home with the owner's family.

Sadly, in today's world it's unclear what being a faithful steward-leader should look like Monday through Saturday while at work. However, the Bible is full of examples of men who proved to be faithful stewards and leaders on the job. Abraham, the father of the Jewish nation, was a free-grazer who followed God west and built a ranching empire on the open range. Joseph started in the family ranching business but ended up the secretary of agriculture and homeland security in the most powerful government of his generation. We usually call Daniel a prophet, but he also was chief of staff for several powerful kings. David was a hymn writer but never received a royalty check from a recording company. He made his living as a military commander and later as the chief executive of Israel. Nehemiah was chief of staff to the king of Persia, and he became the general contractor for the rebuilding of Jerusalem's wall.

Jesus Himself was no stranger to the workplace, laboring as a carpenter until He began His ministry. Forty-five of Jesus' fifty-two parables had a workplace context.

In Colossians 3 and 4, Paul writes at length about our work-life habits. In the cities where Paul ministered, the average business staff was made up of slaves and masters. Note how he addresses the management and labor issues of his day.

> *Slaves, obey your earthly masters in everything; and do it, not only when their eye is on you and to win their favor, but with sincerity of heart and reverence for the Lord. Whatever you do, work at it with all your heart, as working for the Lord, not for men, since you know that you will receive an inheritance from the Lord as a reward. It is the Lord Christ you are serving. Anyone who does wrong will be repaid for his wrong, and there is no favoritism.*
>
> *Masters, provide your slaves with what is right and fair, because you know that you also have a Master in heaven.*
>
> *Devote yourselves to prayer, being watchful and thankful. And pray for us, too, that God may open a door for our message, so that we may proclaim the mystery of Christ, for which I am in chains. Pray that I may proclaim it clearly, as I should. Be wise in the way you act toward outsiders; make the most of every opportunity. Let your conversation be always full of grace, seasoned with salt, so that you may know how to answer everyone.* Colossians 3:22–4:6

In this passage, Paul gives us five specific ways our faith should influence our work.

1. We are to have an attitude of service. The world says we must have power. But note the contrast: God says we go to work not to get others to serve us but to serve them. Not to gain power for ourselves, but to empower others. This applies to everyone, no matter where we are on the corporate food chain. According to Paul, whether we are giving or taking orders, we are to take the lead in seeking the welfare and success of others. Whether I am an employee or an employer, manager or the managed, Paul says I go to work not primarily for myself, but for others. I am to treat the person for whom I work fairly, doing the work that is expected of me. As for those who work for me, I am to act fairly and empower them to do their work. We are to be proactive—not waiting to be served but taking the initiative to serve.

As the owner of a dozen McDonald's restaurants in Colorado, Steve Bigari takes his responsibility to love and serve his employees in Jesus' name seriously. He is a hero in my book and also to the Colorado Springs Chamber of Commerce, which recently named Steve Business Citizen of the Year. When I met Steve in 2003, his passion for Jesus, his business, and his five hundred or so employees was obvious. He was determined to help his hourly wage earners become successful citizens. His method: love them in Jesus' name and provide them the tools they need to stay employed—health care, transportation, child care, and education. He offered benefits to workers at the bottom of the wage scale, which is rare in fast-food franchises. Today, Steve has realized a dream in the establishment of America's Family, a nonprofit organization that spreads what Steve has learned to other hardworking Americans beyond his business.[1]

2. **We are to do our work with integrity.** Paul's words *with sincerity* literally mean "without wax." This common image from his day refers to how dishonest potters would repair damage done in the kiln to a piece of pottery by filling in cracks with wax. Paul exhorts us to be straightforward in all our actions rather than dishonest like these potters. Whether someone is

watching or not, our work should be of superior quality, nothing hidden. The fact is, since Jesus is the Lord of the workplace we are always being watched anyway.

3. **We are to do our work with excellence.** We are to put our whole heart into it, according to Paul. The Lord of the workplace deserves it, as do our fellow men. Remember Dorothy Sayers's words on page 151, "What the Church should be telling him [an intelligent carpenter] is this: that the first demand that his religion makes upon him is that he should make good tables."[2] When my son Joel began his business, he made excellence the high watermark. He named it Hole in the Roof Marketing after the instance in Luke 5 where a group of men go above and beyond to get their paralytic friend to Jesus. Joel's stated operating principle is to provide his customers with creative solutions above and beyond expectation. This commitment to excellence distinguishes his business among his competitors. Pursuing excellence in our work is always the right thing to do. God and men recognize good work when they see it. Besides, can you imagine Jesus turning out a wobbly table? "Do you see a man skilled in his work? He will serve before kings; he will not serve before obscure men" (Proverbs 22:29).

4. **We are to have an attitude of worship as we work.** Eric Liddell might be surprised that millions of people today know his name. He's remembered, not because of the gold medal he won at the 1924 Olympics in Paris or because of his death in a Japanese prison camp in 1945 while serving as a missionary to China. Instead, he gained recent fame because he was the subject of an Academy Award–winning movie. *Chariots of Fire* immortalized his decision to honor God's name by not running in his strongest event, which had been scheduled to be run on a Sunday. Liddell, like most serious Christians of his day, felt participating in sports activities on the "Sabbath" violated the command of God. By choosing not to run, he subordinated his chance to make a name for himself so he could honor God's name. Honor-

ing God was paramount in everything that Liddell did, whether running the 400 meters or pursuing his ministry.

The world says we must strive for prestige. We've got to make a name for ourselves. But God says we go to work, not to make a name for ourselves, but to make a name for God. Paul makes it clear that work is at its core a means of worship, that is, ascribing worth to God—"It is the Lord Christ you are serving."

Don't miss how scandalous these words must have sounded to Greek ears. Paul says that *whatever* you do *can* and *is* to be done for the Lord. It is hard to escape the idea that Paul sees all work as meaningful and God honoring. Considering that Paul is addressing slaves, some of whom no doubt did the most menial labor, his words are even more shocking. *Whatever* includes a substantial variety of unpleasant activities. Paul's words strike a deathblow to the idea that God's work and one's daily work are separate categories. All work is God's work. If you are meeting legitimate human needs, you are working for God. As we saw in an earlier chapter, work is what we were created to do, and when we do it well, as an act of love and worship "as unto the Lord," our work glorifies the God whom we serve.

> *Lord, help me do great things as though they were little, since I do them with Your powers; and help me to do little things as though they were great, because I do them in Your Name.*
>
> BLAISE PASCAL

5. **We are to have an attitude of expectation.** The world says you must have possessions. It's about the money! But God says we go to work, not primarily to make a living, but to earn an eternal reward. My daily work counts for eternity. Paul clearly teaches that God will hold us accountable as stewards for what we do in our daily work. He desires to give us our heart's desire, but in a way that we might not expect.

The profit motive runs strong within us. That's what makes money dangerous. But far from condemning our desire to profit from our work, the Bible redirects us to remember the ultimate reward for good labor. In his insightful essay "The Weight of Glory," C. S. Lewis suggests that God finds our desire for profit too small, not too large. "We are," as he says, "far too easily pleased" with worldly things, when what we really want is waiting for us before God.

> It is written that we shall "stand before" Him, shall appear, shall be inspected. The promise of glory is the promise, almost incredible and only possible by the work of Christ, that some of us, that any of us who really chooses, shall actually survive that examination, shall find approval, shall please God. To please God . . . to be a real ingredient in the divine happiness . . . to be loved by God, not merely pitied, but delighted in as an artist delights in his work or a father in a son—it seems impossible, a weight or burden of glory which our thoughts can hardly sustain. But so it is.[3]

Implications for Our Lives

Here's the sum of what Paul is saying in Colossians 3 about our work. First, we can make any job secular or sacred by our attitude. Apart from something sinful, whatever we do can be done for God. What is important here is not so much *what* we do, but *why* we do it and for *whom* we do it. That means that we can actually take work that is traditionally considered sacred, God-honoring, and valuable to the Kingdom—prayer, evangelism, Bible study, serving the poor—and actually secularize it by our attitude. As I confessed earlier, I turned teaching God's Word into secular work by tainting it with the desire to make a name for myself. A person can also turn prayer into a self-centered activity designed to manipulate God. Another person might share his faith to get a spiritual notch on his belt or because he feels personally superior to someone with another belief system. Someone else may serve the poor only because it looks good on his résumé.

Actually, we should all go to work for the same reasons we go to church: to worship God, serve our fellow man, and fulfill our stewardship responsibilities. If we go to work for a different reason than our pastor does, one of us is going to work for the wrong reason.

Second, work is not the enemy of our spiritual life. Paul implies something astounding here that we shouldn't miss: "Whatever you do, work at it with all your heart as unto the Lord." This admonition is often at odds, not only with the world's attitudes, but with more than a few churches where daily work is portrayed as a distraction—something that competes head-on with family life, church life, and especially one's personal spiritual life. The truth is, if work is the enemy of these other areas of life, then it's difficult if not impossible to be serious both about your work and about serving God at the same time. In contrast to this mind-set, Paul sees work as a part of daily life as well as an essential part of the spiritual life. Those who want to divide life into the secular and the sacred have a real problem making Paul's words in Colossians 3:23 fit with Jesus' statement in Matthew 22:37-38: "'Love the Lord your God with all your heart and with all your soul and with all your mind.' This is the first and greatest commandment."

If you keep work separated from your spiritual life, how can you spend 40 to 60 percent of your waking hours putting "all your heart" into your work as Paul commands, and loving the Lord with "all your heart" as Jesus commands? You can't obey one command without disobeying the other.

> *Every man's work, whether it be literature, or music, or pictures, or architecture, or anything else, is always a portrait of himself.*
>
> SAMUEL BUTLER

On the other hand, if you view your work as God's work and work at it with all your heart to bring glory to God, then your work can be a supreme act of love and worship of God. In Paul's mind, a man is hard pressed to please God apart from a healthy attitude toward work. Personally, I think it is impossible to bring life into proper balance apart from viewing work as important to God. If I believed that God cares nothing about the part of my life where I spend the bulk of my waking hours, then not only am I totally on my own at work, but God is simply an add-on option to my life. He is something I may or may not choose to make room for in my leisure time. I will not view my relationship with God as essential, nor will I depend on Him in my work. That puts everything on my shoulders, which as any man knows, makes it hard to walk away from work at the end of the day to tend to other responsibilities of stewardship. In this case, *my attitude* about work does become the enemy of my spiritual life, and it becomes impossible to keep my work in balance with other important activities of life.

A New Source of Power

If we are going to keep work in proper balance and accomplish what God desires, we will need serious help. That's why Paul writes,

> *Devote yourselves to prayer, being watchful and thankful. And*
> *pray for us, too, that God may open a door for our message,*
> *so that we may proclaim the mystery of Christ, for which I am*
> *in chains. Pray that I may proclaim it clearly, as I should.*
> Colossians 4:2-4

Paul's words here are often taken as a break from the preceding verses on work ("Whatever you do, work at it with all your heart, as working for the Lord. . . ."). However, I believe they continue to refer to his readers' workplace setting. Verse 2 is a bridge from the Colossian reader's workplace to Paul's present work "assignment." Paul is reminding his readers we must all do our work, not in our own strength, but in God's.

I remember a man once asking me, "Do you think it's okay to pray about a business decision?" I was a little shocked at the question, but from the look on the questioner's face, I knew he was sincere. This man had been a Christian since childhood, was active in his church, and was committed to ministry to the poor in his city. His question, however, told me he didn't understand the stewardship responsibility he had with his business.

Paul says prayer is something we are to be *devoted* to. The word Paul uses means "to attend to constantly." I don't know about you, but I don't attend constantly to anything that I don't think is absolutely critical. Evidently that's how Paul looked at prayer. The word *devote* itself gives us a clue why.

The word Paul uses is a compound word made up of the Greek word for *unto* plus the word that means *strength, might,* and *dominion.* It carries the idea of leaning into a source of power. It expresses a very concrete act of trust, reliance, and dependence. In so many words, Paul is saying that God is our source of power. We are to ask for it and depend on Him—not on our business skills or our bank account, but on God Himself. Prayer is our declaration of dependence on God for both our spiritual and economic welfare.

We need God's power for everything we do. If ever there was a person who by sheer force of personality could have done his work on his own, it was Paul. He was a leader driven to overcome and prevail over any opponent, adversary, or obstacle. But when Paul considered his work, he knew nothing happened without God. So we find him repeatedly requesting prayer.

You may think, *Well, of course, I understand that. To accomplish "spiritual" results, you need prayer.* If you are still wondering how appropriate it is to pray, say, for a business result, consider this. In His last conversation with His disciples, Jesus told them that the Father's will was for them to bear much fruit. And He made it clear how this would be accomplished. He said, "I am the vine; you are the branches. If a man remains in me and I in him, he will bear much fruit; apart from me you can do nothing" (John 15:5). In other words, we accomplish nothing on our own. We are fruitful to the extent we are filled with Jesus' power.

Bible teachers have argued ad nauseum over what kind of fruit Jesus was talking about here. One will argue the fruit is *godly character,* i.e. the fruit of the Spirit. Others argue that the fruit Jesus was talking about is *souls saved.* But we know from Genesis 1 that God commanded us to be fruitful on a much broader level. Fruit is any good thing God wants for His creation—physically,

> *Faith is the daring of the soul to go farther than it can see.*
>
> WILLIAM NEWTON CLARKE

socially, spiritually, emotionally, or economically. We pray because apart from Jesus we can do nothing that honors Him, whether it's growing spiritually, influencing friends and colleagues to trust Christ, building a business, or consistently doing good work. It's all part of God's grand design for His kingdom, and we need His power to accomplish it. If you really believed that God was the essential ingredient in every activity of your daily life and business, how would that make a difference in the content and frequency of your prayers?

A New Career Objective

Paul wants us to consider one more reason our work can be rich with meaning, and it flies in the face of the world's view of work. We go to work not to climb a ladder, but to walk through open doors. In Paul's closing instructions to the Colossians, he exhorts them not to miss the opportunity:

> Be wise in the way you act toward outsiders; make the most of every opportunity. Let your conversation be always full of grace, seasoned with salt, so that you may know how to answer everyone. Colossians 4:5-6

We'll look at this passage in greater detail in the next chapter, but for now just take a few moments to consider Paul's words. Every Monday morning when you go to work, you walk into the most strategic mission field in the world. Your workplace, as much as the Colosse marketplace of Paul's day, is where God wants people to see the gospel lived out before their eyes. God does not rely on stadium events, mass media, or superstar Christians to spread the gospel, but on men (and women) who are willing to take their faith to work—whether it's to a first-century bakery or a twenty-first-century bank. Note that our job is less about bringing people to Jesus than it is about bringing Jesus to people. We are His hands and His heart to the people who cross our path in the course of daily business—as we do our work with an attitude of service and worship, empowered by His Spirit at work within us.

Living as a Faithful Steward

God's business interests don't stop when we drive out of the church parking lot on Sunday. He expects us to serve Him well in all of our work activities and to make Him known in the workplace as well. Paul's exhortation in Colossians 3:17 is a good one for all of us to post in our mind for easy reference: "And whatever you do, whether in word or deed, do it all in the name of the Lord Jesus, giving thanks to God the Father through him."

If this is our modus operandi, when our work on earth is done, we'll hear our Master say, "Well done."

1. How would you do your daily work differently if you knew God cared about what you did and why you did it?

2. What do you see as the biggest difficulties in taking your faith to work? What would be the disadvantages? What would be the advantages?

3. When people watch you do your work, can they tell that you are working by a different value system? How would they know?

4. What can you do to transform your work into an experience of worship?

5. What help do you need from others to "do your work as unto the Lord"?

6. What is one thing for which you would like someone to join you in prayer concerning your work?

13

Stewards of the Message

> The best argument for Christianity is Christians: their joy, their certainty, their completeness. But the strongest argument against Christianity is also Christians—when they are somber and joyless, when they are self-righteous and smug in complacent consecration—when they are narrow and repressive, then Christianity dies a thousand deaths.   SHELDON VANAUKEN

The greatest communication success story in human history is how the gospel message spread across the Mediterranean world. Followers of Jesus grew from a few hundred on the day of Pentecost to more than six million people by the end of the second century.[1] That's an amazing number, considering the only media were word-of-mouth encounters and hand-written letters—their delivery schedule giving new meaning to the term *snail mail*. It's tempting to assume that the growth of the church at this time was due to the effective preaching of Peter, Paul, and a few other gifted communicators. After all, the apostles planted churches in key cultural centers, and these churches then spread to the countryside. Yet while their efforts were important, more important was the attitude of ordinary Christians, who recognized that sharing the message of Jesus was everyone's mission. The gospel spread like wildfire from house to house (oikos to *oikos*)—as men and women personally gossiped the gospel to friends, relatives, acquaintances, colleagues, masters, slaves, students, teachers, customers, shop owners, and fellow soldiers in their everyday networks.

In the mid 1970s, Kathy and I had the privilege of watching this kind of "*oikos* evangelism" at work. Our friends Tom and Ann met at Texas Christian University and married after graduation. Although both Tom and Ann had been nominally religious growing up, they had never understood the gospel message. Over a number of months—at social gatherings, business lunches, and children's activities—friends casually and naturally introduced Tom and Ann to Christ, and they began to grow in their faith. But that was only the beginning of the story.

Thankfully, unlike many Christians who feel they must quit their jobs and enroll in seminary or become a missionary to be used by God, no one told Tom and Ann that evangelism was for trained professionals. They just began sharing Christ in the same way they had been introduced to Him, living winsomely and building curiosity in the lives of their friends by what they said and did. People saw how Tom and Ann's lives began to change, which provided natural opportunities for them to explain what Christ had done for them. Tom talked about his faith naturally and casually to his colleagues at work, and when someone showed a little interest, he and Ann invited them into their world—to dinner, football games, and community events where they also introduced them to other Christian friends. Over time, these friends began to respond to Christ and joined Tom and Ann in sharing Jesus with other friends—*oikos* to *oikos*—in their own network of relationships. So the gospel traveled not over the airwaves, but from person to person, house to house, workplace to workplace, network to network, and throughout Fort Worth. Today, over thirty years later, many hundreds of men and women can trace their spiritual roots back to friends and work associates—and ultimately to Tom and Ann.

In a day when our culture is moving further away from Christ with increasing speed, we might assume that reaching people with the gospel has gotten harder. In one way this is true in that it's harder to get people to visit a church, listen to a gospel presentation, or attend an evangelistic crusade. But the avenue of personal relationships remains wide open. As uninterested and even hostile as people may seem today toward the kind of Christianity they often see portrayed in the media, millions are thirsty for spiritual refreshment. George Barna uncovered this thirst in his research.

> Our surveys consistently detect a large (and growing) majority of adults who are dissatisfied and are searching for something more meaningful than bigger homes, fatter paychecks, trimmer bodies, more erotic affairs, and extended leisure. Tens of millions of Americans are open to a set of spiritual truths that will set them free from the shackles of worldliness.[2]

But it's not just the opportunity created by people's thirst that should motivate us. The spreading of the gospel message is every man's responsibility. It's our job and a responsibility Paul felt personally: "Let a man regard us in this manner, as servants of Christ and stewards of the mysteries of God. In this case, moreover, it is required of stewards that one be found trustworthy" (1 Corinthians 4:1-2 NASB).

All of us who have received the gospel share this stewardship with Paul—no matter what our vocation.

My friend Steve traveled a long way to learn this lesson. He went somewhat reluctantly on a short-term mission trip down the Amazon. Three days into the journey, the team leader asked him to share his testimony at a gathering in a fishing village along the river. Working with an interpreter, Steve overcame his fear, and when villagers responded to Steve's presentation of the gospel, his life made a one-eighty.

The key to evangelism is not a technique. It's not a format. It's not communication skills. It's first and foremost a fire that burns in us.
REBECCA PIPPERT

You see, his wife had talked him into going on the trip in hopes that the experience would rekindle the joy that had been missing in his life since the death of their son. Steve had been acting comatose at church, and any spiritual conversation between the two of them would last about forty-five seconds tops. But on Steve's return, she wondered if her plan may have produced more change than she had bargained for. As she listened to his stories and saw his changed life, she realized that becoming a missionary wife was a distinct possibility—not part of her plan.

Steve felt a strong pull to the mission field and even filled out a seminary application, but before he quit his work as an Internet entrepreneur, he discovered that he could and actually wanted to talk about spiritual things with the men and women with whom he worked—and they were interested in hearing about what happened on his trip. His eyes were opened to the opportunity all around him.

When I had the opportunity to sit down with Steve, I explained to him that following Jesus is more about a heart change than a career change. God could certainly call him to the mission field, but first God wanted him to be a missionary right where he was with the people at his workplace and his network of relationships—his *oikos*. Steve's mission trip was a wakeup call, not only to his spiritual life, but to the mission field where he lived.

Many Christians miss this fact, ignoring their most significant mission field. Just before Jesus departed the earth, he gave these marching orders to his disciples. "But you will receive power when the Holy Spirit comes on you; and you will be my witnesses in Jerusalem, and in all Judea and Samaria, and to the ends of the earth" (Acts 1:8).

In this short strategic plan to take the gospel to the human race, Jesus made it clear that His plan included the entire planet. But, the retaking of the planet began with the people in closest proximity to His followers. Jesus describes four mission fields that can be graphed along two axes: cultural proximity and geographical proximity.

YOUR JERUSALEM (culturally and geographically close): Neighbors and work associates fit into this group. This is where Tom and Ann and Steve found their most significant mission field.

YOUR JUDEA (culturally similar but geographically more distant): Tom and Ann weren't able to connect daily with long-distance family and friends, yet they continued to pray for them and reach out as they were able.

	GEOGRAPHICALLY FAR	
JUDEA The men and women out of our direct contact who are culturally similar: people and groups with whom we share common language and heritage		**ENDS OF THE EARTH** People and groups who are more or less distant both culturally and geographically: men and women reached through global mission partnerships and global commerce
CULTURALLY SIMILAR		**CULTURALLY DIFFERENT**
JERUSALEM The men and women with whom we have direct contact: family, neighbors, colleagues, clients, and work associates		**SAMARIA** People and groups who are relatively close geographically but culturally distant: the poor and underserved, various ethnic groups, immigrants, and refugees in our community
	GEOGRAPHICALLY NEAR	

YOUR SAMARIA (culturally different but geographically within reach): Every community today has a group of disenfranchised people who need ministry. Steve Bigari, the McDonald's owner whom I introduced in chapter 12, founded America's Family because of his concern for hardworking low-income employees.

YOUR ENDS OF THE EARTH (culturally and geographically distant): This group includes people you can only reach via short-term mission trips, global initiatives, and mission partnerships in cultures all over the world. Steve learned just how rewarding—even life-changing—this type of ministry can be during his Amazon trip.

Many people are surprised to learn that 70 to 90 percent of people who come to Christ do so because of a relationship with a friend or relative. When I ask men what comes to mind when I say the word evangelism, many say, "Billy Graham." While he is certainly a gifted evangelist, Graham's model is not one most followers of Jesus can embrace for themselves with confidence. Fortunately, God has not left us in the dark about what He expects of us as stewards of His grace. At the end of his letter to the Colossians Paul gives some important instructions that clear up a lot of confusion about the spiritual influence God expects of us. He writes:

> Devote yourselves to prayer, being watchful and thankful. And pray for us, too, that God may open a door for our message, so that we may proclaim the mystery of Christ, for which I am in chains. Pray that I may proclaim it clearly, as I should.
> Be wise in the way you act toward outsiders; make the most of every opportunity. Let your conversation be always full of grace, seasoned with salt, so that you may know how to answer everyone. Colossians 4:2-6

Nestled in these verses are four important principles of spiritual leadership we can take with us when we go to work.

1. Every interaction with a non-Christian is an opportunity for spiritual influence. The persecution that the first-century followers of Jesus faced could easily have kept the gospel contained in a tight little enclave of a religious community. Doubtless, many who heard and received the gospel were fearful and kept the gospel to themselves. But overall, Christians understood that from the one who is given much, much is required. And as they went through their day, doing their work and interacting with people in their community, they looked for opportunities to talk about what Jesus was doing for them.

Evangelism that ignores wooing and tries to force a union misses the very heart of the new life in and with Jesus Christ. . . . Give the Bridegroom plenty of time to do His courting.

JUDY GOMBOLL

A lot of people try to make evangelism something way too complicated—something they must have hours of training to do. At least part of the reason they think this way is because they have a picture of evangelism that entails persuading reluctant strangers to believe something they really don't want to believe. The sign-up line for this kind of evangelism is pretty short. But if you think about evangelism as a process (as I describe it below), it becomes much less threatening. Certainly our words are important and we need to be able to talk intelligently about our faith and the facts of the gospel, but sophisticated arguments are not necessary when the men and women we interact with at work see the reality of our faith lived out every day.

One of the ways I love to bring faith into a conversation is through what I call a "faith flag," a simple one or two sentence statement about God or the Bible that lets someone know that I take faith seriously. A faith flag should always be pertinent and a natural part of the conversation. For example, when talking with someone who is discouraged, you might say, "Last year I was so discouraged. A friend suggested I read some passages in the Bible and it really helped." Or if you are complimenting someone on their good work you might say something like, "You seem to have a gift from God to handle difficult people."[3]

2. **Spiritual influence begins with prayer.** While we ought always to improve our skills in sharing our faith, spiritual influence is more about what God is doing than what we do.

The early church was highly successful in spreading the gospel, not only because of the mass mobilization of street-level Christians, but because of the persistent prayer of the early Christians. They believed prayer was essential to their mission. Over and over again Paul asked the churches to pray for him. He understood the critical role of the Holy Spirit in spreading the gospel.

> *Pray also for me, that whenever I open my mouth, words may be given me so that I will fearlessly make known the mystery of the gospel, for which I am an ambassador in chains. Pray that I may declare it fearlessly, as I should.* Ephesians 6:19-20

Paul knew that the door into the human heart will remain locked and bolted from within without prayer. He also knew that if we want to talk to men effectively for God, we need to first talk with God about men.

3. **Spiritual influence is incremental.** Early in my Christian life I developed the impression that evangelism is an event. I've since learned it is not: It is a process. Yet this misunderstanding of evangelism as an event has sidelined many Christians—myself included—who failed miserably at aggressive evangelism. Christians who thought they needed to pressure a friend or coworker into accepting Christ have unintentionally alienated thousands if not millions of pre-Christians. Unfortunately, these people learned to run the other way from anyone they feared might broach a spiritual conversation. And why not? The fear of being put into a spiritual corner is typically not too high on anyone's Most Pleasant Experiences list.

> *Conversion is a process. . . . Few of us make it in one big decision. Instead, it is a multitude of small choices—mini-decisions that a person makes toward Christ.*
>
> JIM PETERSEN

For most people, the path to faith is a long-term process and usually involves several people over what can seem to be a long time. I like to call this organic evangelism because it is how Jesus described the process to His disciples. Lest they misunderstand and inflate their own contribution to the spiritual harvest in Samaria, Jesus told them that others had already done the hard work—the cultivation of hearts. "Thus the saying 'One sows and another reaps' is true. I sent you to reap what you have not worked for. Others have done the hard work, and you have reaped the benefits of their labor" (John 4:37-38).

The goal of evangelism is to see men and women place their trust in Christ. But just like a farmer's field, the human heart usually needs a lot of preparation. That preparation can't be done at a distance—there's no tele-(at a distance) evangelism in the New Testament. It requires working up close and personal over time.

Most men and women need to see the authenticity of our faith to know they can trust the gospel message and the Savior it proclaims. Before deciding that the gospel message is reliable, our coworkers need to hear it explained and see it lived out. Except in rare instances, this will not happen after one encounter with one individual. The average journey to faith involves nine to sixteen individuals who help a non-Christian take incremental steps that finally lead to faith in Christ and continued spiritual growth.

4. **Spiritual influence involves words *and* deeds.** Interestingly the Bible never commands—or even asks us—to go witnessing. It does, however, make it very clear that we are Christ's witnesses. The word witness (the noun, not the verb) pervades the New Testament. Witnessing (the verb) dominates our perception of evangelism.

Unlike witnessing, being a witness is not something we do, but who we are, whether good or bad and whether we like it or not. Paul describes the kind of witness who attracts people to Christ in Colossians 4:5-6. Note that actions precede words in his instructions. "Be wise in the way you *act* toward outsiders" (emphasis mine).

Paul's words seem to indicate that there is a cause-effect relationship between words and deeds. Gracious acts, followed by our gracious conversation, creates a curiosity in people who observe us in daily life. Their curiosity often prompts them to ask us about our beliefs, opening a door for us to explain the hope and joy we have in Christ.

In 1 Peter 3 the cause-effect is even clearer. "In your hearts set apart Christ as Lord. Always be prepared to give an answer to everyone who asks you to give the reason for the hope that you have. But do this with gentleness and respect" (1 Peter 3:15).

So what is it that makes a person ask? What is it that causes men and women to be curious about our faith? The answer is in the verses preceding verse 15.

Finally, all of you, live in harmony with one another; be sympathetic, love as brothers, be compassionate and humble.

Do not repay evil with evil or insult with insult, but with blessing, because to this you were called so that you may inherit a blessing. . . . Who is going to harm you if you are eager to do good? But even if you should suffer for what is right, you are blessed. "Do not fear what they fear; do not be frightened." 1 Peter 3:8-14

Note first that how we treat other people is critically important. The quality of our relationships determines the quality of our influence.

Second, we must be people of godly character. People become interested in Jesus when they see Jesus in us. Both what we say and what we do reveal what is in our hearts.

Third, we must do good work. The good Peter says we are to do in verse 13 is not just "good deeds" but all the good work we do every day, whether it's closing a deal or doing the dishes, mucking out a barn or changing a diaper, studying a contract or studying for an exam.

Living as a Faithful Steward

A number of times I have referred to William Wilberforce. If you recall, Wilberforce had two great objectives in his life, not only to abolish the slave trade, but also to "reform English manners" (or, as we would say today, moral values). At the end of the eighteenth century, England was a moral mess. According to historian John Pollock:

Too many people were being hanged. Venality, drunkenness, and the high crime rate arose from the general decadence, especially the corruption and irreligion of the trendsetters, not in those days pop stars and media moguls but the nobility and landed gentry. The "high civilization" of the eighteenth century England was built on the Slave Trade, mass poverty, child labor, and political corruption in high places.[4]

Wilberforce knew that legislation alone would never bring the deep soul change needed to change society. A change of moral fiber would demand a spiritual foundation. Only a movement of the gospel in the human heart would do that. As it is in our day, the evangelical faith was out of fashion among cultural leaders, and those serious about their faith were considered feeble minded. Sound familiar? The spiritual awakening led by George Whitfield and John Wesley that swept England in the mid-eighteenth century had been largely confined to the lower classes. Wilberforce determined to spread the gospel to his peers and led dozens of influential Britons to Christ. The result of this person-to-person spreading of the faith changed England. By the mid-nineteenth century, goodness became "fashionable" as a result of a great blooming of the Christian faith in hearts and minds in England.

Like Wilberforce, you and I have the opportunity to spread the gospel to our peers—the men and women with whom we live and work daily. I encourage you to begin with your "Jerusalem," just as Wilberforce did.

1. Look back at the Acts 1:8 chart on page 169. Name some people in each group who come to mind. What opportunities do you have to touch them with Christ's love?

2. How many Christians do you work with in your workplace? Are the non-Christians in your workplace attracted or repelled by them? Why?

3. Think of the people who played a role in your spiritual journey. Share with your group some of the key individuals and how they affected you.

4. What are the things you saw in others that attracted you to consider Christ?

5. Read 1 Peter 3:15 again. What important principles do you learn from this passage?

6. Does your life attract others to Christ? What needs to change? If you told the people you work with that you are a follower of Jesus, what would they say? Would they be surprised? Would they want to know more about your faith?

A word of warning: No one wants to be someone's spiritual project. If you just want to put another notch on your evangelistic belt, your coworkers will sniff it out in an instant and the odor won't be pleasant to them. Stop and check your motives. No one has squeaky clean motives, but do you really care about the people you're praying for?

He is the richest man who enriches his country most; in whom the people feel richest and proudest; who gives himself with his money; who opens the doors of opportunity widest to those about him; who is ears to the deaf, eyes to the blind, and feet to the lame. Such a man makes every acre of land in his community worth more, and makes richer every man who lives near him.

ORISON SWETT MARDEN, American author and founder of *Success* magazine

We have attempted to transform our cities for years without success. I now believe the reason is because pastors and church leaders do not have the authority to do so. That authority lies within those leaders in the marketplace. When we recognize and affirm the apostles in the marketplace we will begin to see the transformation of cities.

DR. PETER WAGNER

I long to accomplish a great and noble task, but it is my chief duty to accomplish humble tasks as though they were great and noble. The world is moved along not only by the mighty shoves of its heroes, but by the aggregate of the tiny pushes of each honest worker.

HELEN KELLER

CHAPTER 14

A Leader's Place in the World

All great systems, ethical or political, attain their ascendancy over the minds of men by virtue of their appeal to the imagination; and when they cease to touch the chords of wonder and mystery and hope, their power is lost, and men look elsewhere for some set of principles by which they may be guided.   RUSSELL KIRK

When was the last time you picked up the paper or watched the evening news and felt good about what was going on in our country? As men, we instinctively want to do something. Do we fight for social justice? work to improve our schools? help the poor? feed the hungry? run for public office? Sorting through so many options—from so many voices and perspectives—can be paralyzing. In the end, many of us throw up our hands and simply sit back to watch the growing decay on the evening news.

No matter where you stand on the issue—or how confused, powerless, and disconnected you may feel—passivity is not an option. We all have a responsibility to influence our world in some way. When we were born spiritually into God's family, we took on a new citizenship in the Kingdom of God. But we're still citizens of earth and of our nation as well. So how do we maintain two allegiances—to God's Kingdom and to the earth on which we live—and keep them in proper balance? There are several well-tried answers that don't work.

Three Classic Mistakes Men Make with the Culture
Assimilation

Perhaps the biggest temptation is allowing ourselves to be engulfed by the culture. The pull of culture on men is irresistible apart from the grace of God. Paul graphically describes this in Ephesians 2.

> *As for you, you were dead in your transgressions and sins, in which you used to live when you followed the ways of this world and of the ruler of the kingdom of the air, the spirit who is now at work in those who are disobedient. All of us also lived among them at one time, gratifying the cravings of our sinful nature and following its desires and thoughts. Like the rest, we were by nature objects of wrath.* Ephesians 2:1-3

Even as Christ followers, breaking free from the clutches of culture is a lifelong struggle. In fact, most Christians give up trying to resist. One of the great tragedies of the church is that faith is often relegated to the private, personal area of life because it's just too complicated and controversial to live as a 24/7 follower of Jesus.

When George Barna surveyed and compared the behavior of Christians and non-Christians, he discovered some alarming trends. He found that most Americans who profess Christianity don't act significantly different in their daily lives from non-Christians. Sadly those who attend church are just as likely as the unchurched to engage in unethical behavior.[1]

To our shame, many who claim to be Christians in America have assimilated into the culture—so much so that we cannot be recognized. Increasingly, the only difference between Christians and their non-Christian neighbors, business associates, or friends is where they spend Sunday mornings.

Isolation

In order to avoid this contamination, some Christians try to opt out of culture altogether, attempting to isolate themselves from it instead of striving to be a fragrant aroma of Christ in the midst of it.

Interestingly, even as Christians have retreated from the culture at large, we've created our own subculture—with mixed results. As author Kary Oberbrunner points out:

We have Christian programming everywhere. . . . Yet, I wonder, what's the effect? Do we have a false sense of victory? Is the world a better place? Are we winning the battle because there is now Christian candy? . . .

Is our goal reached when we participate in every aspect of the market by providing a Christian alternative? It seems to me that all these alternatives collectively produce one common outcome. It seems they create a subculture that separates us further from the very people we are trying to reach. I don't recall God giving us the option to create an alternative subculture that retreats and hides out from the world.[2]

Take-over

In the late 1970s, many Christians shrugged off their cultural lethargy and emerged as a political force, rightly emphasizing their responsibility as citizens. Christian leaders began to call followers of Christ to assert their political will by voting for candidates who held Christian values.

But a problem emerged. A number of Christian leaders began to master the tools of political power and became more obsessed with winning arguments, elections, and media space than they were about seizing the imagination of fellow citizens with God's grace. Although elections were won, the rhetoric coming from the Christian right was sometimes shrill and mean-spirited, and far from honoring to Christ.

There is a huge difference between exerting godly influence on civil affairs and actually seizing power. In fact, the church has never done well when it has been too closely aligned with government. In the fourth century AD Christianity became the official religion of the Roman Empire under Constantine. The

> *When I became a Christian . . . I began to see that societies are changed only when people are changed, not the other way around.*
> CHUCK COLSON

upside was that persecution of Christians stopped. However, there was a downside. Timothy George notes, "Within a few generations, those who had once been persecuted became persecutors."[3] When the church gets too cozy with the state, religion is politicized and the state is idolized. In the end, Christianity is marginalized. "The danger of being co-opted by forces inimical to the gospel," according to George, "is not limited to one political party or ideology. It can arise from any point along the political spectrum, from the raucous right, the loony left, or the mushy middle."[4]

God Has Plans for the Earth

So how can we avoid the drift into assimilation, the attempt to isolate, or the temptation to try to take over and seize the reigns of power? First, we must recognize our dual citizenship and ask two questions: What is the Master doing in the world? And how does He want me to join him?

1. What is God up to?

Redeeming people. Few evangelical Christians would argue with this. Jesus' own words proclaim clearly that He came to "seek and to save what was lost" (Luke 19:10). Those Christians coming from a liberal theological viewpoint often discount the church's mission to bring spiritual salvation to the world. They have slipped into a theological ditch, denying the need for the atonement and emphasizing instead the social aspects of Jesus' ministry. The Bible is clear, however, that every follower of Jesus is responsible to seek the spiritual welfare of men and women who do not know Christ. "And he has committed to us the message of reconciliation. We are therefore Christ's ambassadors, as though God were making his appeal through us. We implore you on Christ's behalf: Be reconciled to God" (2 Corinthians 5:19-20).

But sadly, while focusing on the world's spiritual needs, evangelicals have slipped into the ditch on the other side of the road, minimizing social responsibility. Following Christ in our age takes us down a road with two lanes of responsibility: the redemption of souls and the redeeming of the earth.

Redeeming the earth. God is clearly interested in the redemption of all His creation. Though it is badly broken, He still claims it as His own. And He has plans for it. "The earth is the LORD's, and everything in it, the world, and all who live in it" (Psalm 24:1).

Most world religions promise their followers deliverance from the physical world. Likewise, a selective reading of the Bible has led some Christians to conclude that the physical world will one day cease to exist and there will be no physical reality to our existence. This is certainly not the view of the Bible. And nowhere in Scripture does God rescind His command to the human race to "be fruitful and increase in number; fill the earth" which we talked about in detail in chapter 3—His original intent for man and creation. Rather, the Bible tells believers our earth will be renewed.

> *The creation waits in eager expectation for the sons of God to be revealed. For the creation was subjected to frustration, not by its own choice, but by the will of the one who subjected it, in hope that the creation itself will be liberated from its bondage to decay and brought into the glorious freedom of the children of God.* Romans 8:19-21

The book of Revelation adds more to this picture of renewal.

> *Then I saw a new heaven and a new earth, for the first heaven and the first earth had passed away, and there was no longer any sea. I saw the Holy City, the new Jerusalem, coming down out of heaven from God, prepared as a bride beautifully dressed for her husband. And I heard a loud voice from the throne saying, "Now the dwelling of God is with men, and he will live with them. They will be his people, and God himself will be with them and be their God. He will wipe every tear from their eyes. There will be no more death or mourning or crying or pain, for the old order of things has passed away." He who was seated on the throne said, "I am making everything new!"* Revelation 21:1-5

Note that in eternity, we will live in a physical place, not as disembodied spirits playing harps and floating on celestial clouds. Note also that this place is a city, and yet the atmosphere sounds very much like the culture we read about in the Garden of Eden—one of peace, harmony, wholeness, health, prosperity, and open fellowship with God. God will return to earth and dwell with men in His creation.

Once we step into eternity, the Great Commission will cease to have relevance since spiritual redemption will have been completed. The cultural mandate of Genesis 1, however, will remain in effect, having never been rescinded. That means that today, we have the continuing responsibility not only to be good stewards of creation, but to seek justice, peace, forgiveness, restoration, and to work toward a healthy society.

2. How do we join Him?

Perhaps the clearest expression of our cultural responsibilities as we live in a sin-dominated society is found in Jeremiah 29.[5] Here's the setting of this important passage. At the turn of the sixth century BC, Babylon invaded and captured the Jewish state. After two Jewish insurrections, Babylon had finally had enough and virtually wiped out the nation. Jerusalem was destroyed, thousands of people were killed, and all but the poorest of the survivors were sent into exile in Babylon. Communicating through the prophet Jeremiah, God told the Jewish exiles how to live in the godless culture they were entering. His instructions to them tell us a lot about how we are to be involved with our community and culture. Here's what we can learn.

God's people should be an engaged counterculture within the community. When the Jewish people arrived in Babylon, they faced a significant temptation to either assimilate or isolate. The Babylonians were masters at luring conquered people into their pluralistic way of life. Rather than enslaving them, they welcomed the young Jewish nobility into their world. A casual reading of the first chapters of the book of Daniel reveals the tremendous temptation these Jews faced on arrival. Rather than physical oppression, the Babylonians offered them the best food, the best education, and positions of influence—as long as they became Babylonian. Everything was calculated to make them Babylonians, intellectually, socially, and spiritually. Rather than antagonizing their defeated enemies like most ancient cultures, the Babylonians absorbed the best and brightest of conquered people into their own culture. This must have seemed almost too good to be true to the demoralized Jews, who had lost everything.

This brilliant strategy meant that the conquered people were in danger of becoming like everyone else; they could lose their identity; and as a result, lose not only their influence but also their will to resist. They were the original melting pot and within a couple of generations, any distinctive identity of the conquered culture would be lost. They would be powerless and devoid of any influence—exactly what the Babylonians wanted.

> *I am only one; but still I am one. I cannot do everything, but still I can do something; I will not refuse to do the something I can do.*
> HELEN KELLER

Still the sophistication, corruption, and idolatry of the Babylonian culture would have repulsed the committed Jews. Furthermore, the natural tendency of any proud people group with a historic culture is to resist the force of assimilation. Because they couldn't resist physically, the Jews' natural strategy to keep themselves pure would have been to insulate themselves as much as possible by isolation. Within their ethnic enclave, men and women could maintain the force of their culture on each other and put forth formidable resistance to acculturation. (A good modern-day example of this is the Amish people of central Pennsylvania.)

It's not surprising that false prophets were encouraging the exiled Jews to isolate. Their message: huddle up, hold on, and take what you need from Babylon to survive. Play the game, but wait—because God would destroy Babylon and bring them home in a couple of years. Not surprisingly, God had a different message for His people. He told them:

> *Build houses and settle down; plant gardens and eat what they produce. Marry and have sons and daughters; find wives for your sons and give your daughters in marriage, so that they too may have sons and daughters. Increase in number there; do not decrease. Also, seek the peace and prosperity of the city to which I have carried you into exile. Pray to the LORD for it, because if it prospers, you too will prosper.* Jeremiah 29:5-7

God's message: Don't assimilate, engage. Increase; don't assimilate. God wanted His people to connect without losing their identity as His people—to maintain their uniqueness without separating so that people could actually see their distinctives.

Jesus reflects this same desire for His disciples. Knowing how hard it would be for His followers to walk the line between assimilation and isolation, on the night before His crucifixion, Jesus prayed for us:

> *I have given them your word and the world has hated them, for they are not of the world any more than I am of the world. My prayer is not that you take them out of the world but that you protect them from the evil one. They are not of the world, even as I am not of it. Sanctify them by the truth; your word is truth. As you sent me into the world, I have sent them into the world.* John 17:14-18

Jesus' desire is for His people to be different, to reflect His holy character and love for them in the way they conduct their lives and in their love for each other. But He also wants us to remain connected enough with the culture so that men and women can see the difference. In the Sermon on the Mount Jesus calls us the light of the world.

> *You are the light of the world. A city on a hill cannot be hidden. Neither do people light a lamp and put it under a bowl. Instead they put it on its stand, and it gives light to everyone in the house. In the same way, let your light shine before men, that they may see your good deeds and praise your Father in heaven.* Matthew 5:14-16

What does this vibrant, light-giving, countercultural community look like? Jesus goes on in the Sermon on the Mount to describe how His followers can reflect this light through the ways they steward marriage, power, and money—ways totally contrary to the ways the world uses these things. Rather than using these things to exploit others, we serve people. Rather than taking, we give. Rather than trying to make a name for ourselves, we live for God's glory.

One of the best examples of this is Chuck Colson, former Nixon staffer and convicted Watergate conspirator. Since he came to faith in Christ, he has poured his energy into and directed his notoriety toward, not only prison reform and redemption of prisoners, but also a number of social justice initiatives.

But there is more, much more. God not only calls us to be an example to the world but to serve the world. Look again at His instructions to the Jews. "Also, seek the peace and prosperity of the city to which I have carried you into exile. Pray to the LORD for it, because if it prospers, you too will prosper" (Jeremiah 29:7).

God's people should be committed to the good of the community. We don't just engage enough to get what we want out of the culture. The culture is to get something out of us as well. We are to pray for our culture, to ask God to bless our city. God told the Jewish exiles to seek the peace of Babylon—the very people who had shattered their peace. *Shalom,* the Hebrew word here translated peace, has an incredibly rich meaning. When we think of peace, we think of the stopping of hostility or our own inner tranquility. Shalom certainly means all of this, but it means far more. When a Jewish person greets you with "Shalom!" he or she is asking God to bless you with wholeness, fulfillment, well-being, harmony, safety, health, and prosperity in every dimension of life—physically, socially, economically, and spiritually. Note also that God wasn't addressing synagogue or religious leaders, but individual citizens. This means that both individually and collectively we should be working for

1. PHYSICAL PEACE—working to provide health care, housing, and protection for the least powerful citizens. If you're a health-care professional, perhaps you could volunteer in a clinic a couple of afternoons a week. Or maybe you could do something on a large scale, like Dr. Ron Anderson, CEO of Parkland Hospital in Dallas and one of the nation's leading advocates of health care for the poor. He established a network of neighborhood-based health centers that act as the "family doctor," primarily to low-income communities. The network includes ten local health centers, eleven school-based clinics, and medical services in twenty-two homeless shelters.

2. SOCIAL PEACE—helping racial and ethnic groups gain status, find reconciliation, and live in harmony. If you are an attorney, maybe you could volunteer at a legal clinic. Since you are reading this book you obviously speak English. That qualifies you to teach English as a Second Language to immigrants in your area. Or maybe you dream of promoting reconciliation like John M. Perkins, who founded Mendenhall Ministries, Voice of Calvary Ministries, and the Christian Community Development Association.

3. ECONOMIC PEACE—raising the economic level of the entire community, making it possible for every family to have economic viability and stability. If you are a business owner, could you hire some international refugees? If you are a banker, could you help your church or inner-city ministry start a micro-lending program in the inner city? Organizations like Opportunity International and Enterprise Development International have been providing loans in third world countries for years. They make loans to nonqualifying individuals other banks won't touch, enabling them to start small businesses.

4. SPIRITUAL PEACE—not only by spreading the gospel but by bringing spiritual wisdom and influence to every institution in the city. You could run for school board or city council, mentor students from inner-city schools, or teach a Bible study in an inner-city neighborhood. You might head up the campaign for your church to sponsor a program such as the one Redeemer Presbyterian Church in Manhattan created called "Hope for the City."

Although Rudy Giuliani is credited with reducing crime and making numerous improvements in New York City's quality of life while he was mayor, perhaps praying Christians under the spiritual leadership of Tim Keller at Redeemer Presbyterian, David Wilkerson of Times Square Church, and Jim Cymbala of Brooklyn Tabernacle had more to do with these changes than meets the eye.

Every man has a different potential for producing peace, depending on the abilities with which God has endowed him, the advantages given by his family, and the doors God opens. If you have access to the political leaders of your community, you can encourage them to work for the welfare of all citizens. Perhaps you'll choose to run for political office yourself or make a street-level investment in your community. For every worker, pursuing peace means doing your best work and caring about your coworkers. For every employer, it means providing employees "what is right and fair." For spiritual leaders, it means teaching spiritual truth and equipping and releasing church members into the community to do the good to which God leads them. For every father, it means loving and staying committed to serve, lead, and provide for his family.

Whatever your level of influence, whatever your opportunity to serve, whatever blessing you are to your community, it will take courage to step out of the comfort of isolation, to resist the temptation to conform, and to give to people who don't have your best interests at heart. But this is our calling.

Historians and sociologists alike have puzzled over how Christianity, once the religion of a small sect of early believers, emerged as the dominant religion in the Roman Empire. A big part of the reason was that every Christian considered himself or herself an evangelist. But there's another side to the story. Sociologist Rodney Stark, in his book *The Rise of Christianity,* suggests that when the cities of the Greco-Roman world were in shambles, ravaged by plague, Christians saw an opening into the culture. Courageous Christians took the opportunity, not to seize power, but to perform the lowliest form of service. Christians stayed in the cities rather than fleeing the plagues. And they took care of dying people—believers and nonbelievers alike—at the cost of their own lives. An eyewitness account, left to us by Bishop Dionysius of Alexandria, reads:

> Most of our brother Christians showed unbounded love and loyalty, never sparing themselves and thinking only of one another. Heedless of danger, they took charge of the sick,

attending to their every need and ministering to them in Christ. . . . Many transferred their death to themselves and died in their stead. The best lost their lives in this manner.[6]

Stark concludes, "The consequence of all of this is that pagan survivors faced greatly increased odds of conversion because of their increased attachments to Christians."[7]

By AD 300 most of the cities of the Roman Empire had large Christian populations. As a result of their "seeking the peace and prosperity of the city," the Christian's Savior captured the imagination of the cities, not because the Christians had tried to gain power but because they gave themselves away.

An Important Reminder

What is it that allows men to abandon our own selfish agendas of self-service and self-satisfaction? We can seek the peace and prosperity of others because we have One who is sovereignly, powerfully, and graciously committed to seeking our peace and prosperity. One can hardly read the entire letter to the Jews in Jeremiah 29 without making the connection. In verse 11, God tells His broken, exiled people: " 'For I know the plans I have for you,' declares the LORD, 'plans to prosper you and not to harm you, plans to give you hope and a future'" (Jeremiah 29:11).

God had asked the Jews to have good intentions toward the Babylonians; clearly He has positive intentions for the Jewish people as well. The word prosper in verse 11 is the same word He used in verse 7, shalom. God's people can seek the peace and prosperity of the city because God seeks our peace and prosperity. No matter how much we might gain or accumulate seeking our own prosperity, we can never experience shalom apart from Jesus. No matter how much we might give away to our community and culture, we will never grow poor with God as our Provider. It's that thought that motivated early Christians to give their lives away during the plagues. It's that thought that will cause us to ask ourselves: *What small act of service can I render that might capture the imagination of men and women I know?*

Living as a Faithful Steward

Before you move on, take a moment to ask what small thing you can do to personally enhance someone's shalom today.

1. How influential are Christians in your community?

2. Of the three mistakes Christian make in responding to culture—assimilation, isolation, takeover—which are you most tempted to fall into?

3. Which of these do you see as most dangerous?

4. How should the church balance the Great Commission with the Cultural Mandate?

5. How do you avoid assimilation if you don't isolate?

6. How are Christians seeking the physical, social, economic, and spiritual peace in your community?

7. Which of these can you make a contribution to?

PART SIX

LEADING AT CHURCH

More than 90 percent of American men believe in God, and five out of six call themselves Christians. But only two out of six attend church on a given Sunday. The average man accepts the reality of Jesus Christ, but fails to see any value in going to church.
DAVID MURROW

There was a time when the church was very powerful. It was during that period when the early Christians rejoiced when they were deemed worthy to suffer for what they believed. In those days the church was not merely a thermometer that recorded the ideas and principles of popular opinion; it was a thermostat that transformed the mores of society.
MARTIN LUTHER KING JR.

Stepping Out of the Pew

> The Church is not a gallery for the exhibition of eminent Christians, but a school for the education of imperfect ones.
> HENRY WARD BEECHER

Recent studies show that the number of men who show up for church on Sundays—much less those who actively participate—is dwindling. Seriously dwindling. Many of the guys who do go to church say they do so to placate their wives. Others won't even go that far. After all, why should they give up prime leisure time to attend a service they can't relate to and hang out with people who don't relate to them?

A whole lot of men feel out of place on Sunday mornings—and women don't understand why. After all, they feel quite comfortable in church, and for the most part, they see men leading the services. They don't see the rub—that if a man goes to church, it's usually because a woman has led him there, not because he's attracted by its relevance to his life. For many guys, church falls into the same category as attending a chick flick with your wife—which I can certainly relate to. I'll never forget the Friday afternoon a few years ago when Kathy and I decided to catch the last matinee of *Mona Lisa Smile*, which she thought might be interesting. When we walked into the theater, I sheepishly looked around and realized there was not another man in sight. The "real men" were in the theater next door enjoying *The Last Samurai*—where I would have rather been. I tried to soothe my insecurity by reminding myself that it was good for me to sacrifice for my wife—not to mention earn some points with her.

For some of you, the idea of going to church to earn points may hit real close to home. Sure, most Sundays you're warming a seat not too far from the front trying to look attentive, but you'd rather be warming a seat in a golf cart, gazing down a fairway. And come spring, you're planning to make your break. Enough is enough! But before you do, before you become part of the male exodus from the church, you need to know that while I sympathize with you, you are opting out of a responsibility that is nonoptional in God's book.

In this chapter I'm going to share some disturbing facts about what the absence of men has done to the church in America today, but first let me remind you of God's intentions for His church as well as for us.

In response to all he has done for us, let us outdo each other in being helpful and kind to each other and in doing good. Let us not neglect our church meetings, as some people do, but encourage and warn each other, especially now that the day of his coming back again is drawing near. Hebrews 10:24-25, TLB

As we approach the end of the first decade of the twenty-first century, the lack of male involvement and the feminization of Christianity have become foregone conclusions by sociologists. While 95 percent of the senior pastors in America are men,[1] women outnumber men in the pews by a substantial proportion—61 percent to 39 percent—and women are 56 percent more likely than men to have held a leadership position (other than pastor) in a congregation.[2] Modern churches, according to Dr. Leon Podles, tend to be "women's clubs with a few male officers."[3]

Work with me here. I do not believe that men's and women's roles are interchangeable in a church family any more than they are in the family. However, my intention is not to debate men's and women's roles in the church, but rather to challenge the male exodus that has caused the church to become overly female friendly at the expense of male involvement—which is detrimental to all and deters the spread of God's Kingdom influence. Men need to feel the call back to their role of steward-leader within the local church.

Other than short intervals of revived male interest, Western Christianity, both Catholic and Protestant, has experienced a 750-

year feminization trend that has become so extreme today that many men consider becoming a Christian a threat to their masculinity. Even if a man moves past the perceived threat and comes to faith, how can the church help him grow into biblical manhood without masculine mentors and an unfeminized version of Jesus—one he can seek to follow as a man? "The sad reality in many churches today is this: *the only man who actually practices his faith is the pastor*," suggests David Murrow, author of *Why Men Hate Going to Church*.[4] Read through the book of Acts, and you will see a different story. Men came to Christ and then brought their entire *oikos* to faith, not the other way around. But don't think a bunch of domineering male leaders ran the early church. Gifted female leaders populate the New Testament too. Mary Magdalene had no problem confronting the apostles' lack of faith. Lydia was the first convert in Europe and opened up her *oikos* to found the first church outside of Asia. Priscilla discipled church leaders and Paul called her a "fellow worker." Phillip had four daughters who exercised the gift of prophecy. Phoebe was singled out as a notable servant of the church. A church met in Nympha's *oikos* in Laodicea. Nowhere do we see heavy-handed males pointing at women and saying, "Submit!" What you do see is both male and female leaders providing balanced leadership together, in ways appropriate to their gender. This no doubt contributed to the success and accelerated growth rate of the early church.

> *The Bible knows nothing of solitary religion.*
> JOHN WESLEY

Why Does the Church Need Men?

It is critically important that the church embrace both masculine and feminine expressions of faith and leadership. How that is done in a particular church or denomination is not the purpose of this book. The point is that when one gender becomes more influential than the other, we reflect a skewed image of God to the world. Today, although most churches are led by men, they are dominated by women, and this imbalance has handicapped the church's mission.

In his book *Why Men Hate Going to Church*, David Murrow describes three gender gaps in the Western church. The first is *presence*. Men are present at church in much smaller numbers than women. The second gap is *participation*. Men simply aren't as involved in or committed to their church. The third gap is *personality*. The church is missing entire personality types that attract men: Risk takers have been replaced by passive types; resolute decision makers by caretakers and bookkeepers.[5]

As men failed to take up their God-given responsibility, the culture and atmosphere of the church shifted toward femininity. Hymns became sentimental and emotionally oriented. Images of a sweet romantic Jesus often dominated. And when there was a need for some spiritual heavy lifting to be done, church professionals took over. No wonder many men think church is dangerous to manhood.

Functional (Not Positional) Leadership

Whether you rarely darken the doors of the church, simply warm a pew, or are heavily involved, I'm not pushing you to seek an official position of leadership in your church, though you may be called to do that. I am, however, at a minimum challenging you to become a *functional* leader, taking the responsibility to manage your own gifts well and invest them to serve the body of Christ in some appropriate way.

Jim attended church for a while before he decided to try to get involved. When he asked about volunteer positions, there weren't any on the list that sounded interesting. He wrote the pastor a note to tell him that he worked at a bank and would like to use his financial skills in some way. The following week Jim was asked to join the finance committee, where he still enjoys serving today. Robert, on the other hand, was a good teacher, but that role wasn't really open to untrained "laymen." He wasn't too jazzed about the greeter position he was given, so he eventually started a men's small group on his own made up of a group of guys from church who worked in his building. They met every other week and together searched for biblical wisdom about the issues they faced at work.

When addressing the churches in the first century, the apostles wrote minimally to those in official church leadership positions and volumes to church members about personal ministry responsibilities, which fell on the *adelphoi* or brothers. To understand their emphasis, *adelphoi,* which usually referred to all male and female believers, is used hundreds of times in the New Testament letters to the churches as opposed to elders (fives times), overseers (four times), and pastors (once).

There's no getting around it. A church simply cannot thrive without male involvement. I'm not talking about men just taking up pew space or showing up to please the women in their lives, or even men filling the official leadership positions. I am talking about men who are willing to take responsibility to use their gifts and, when in a position of responsibility, to lead well.

This is our job. Taking the initiative to act responsibly is nonoptional. Passivity is no more acceptable here than it is in any other relationship. As you step out to fulfill your steward-leader responsibilities in this realm, keep the following principles in mind.

1. **Recognize that people are depending on you.** Soon after I had completed 120 graduate hours of theological study, lost my hair learning Greek and Hebrew, and convinced a church that they should hire this budding theologian, I had lunch with a man who threw cold water on my view of the church and thankfully changed the course of my ministry. This friend, a title attorney from Fort Worth, Texas, sat across from me and casually said, "Bill, God's heroes don't stand behind pulpits." Thirty-plus years later, I know he is right.

   Unfortunately for men, many pastors and church staff think they need to do the important spiritual tasks. One guy told me that every time he works on an important project at church, he reaches a point where someone on the church staff basically tells him, "We'll take it from here." That attitude is not only unbiblical, it cuts the spiritual life out of a man. In far too many churches, men are relegated to bantam-weight tasks when they have the capacity to be the heroes and spiritual giants.

Every member of the body of Christ is gifted and responsible to make some contribution to the group of believers with whom he fellowships. Don't think that just because females tend to volunteer more quickly or your church hires paid staff to handle the "important" spiritual tasks that you can sit back and relax. You read in chapter 6 that your God-given gifts came with a responsibility attached, and God holds you accountable to use those gifts, whether or not you feel comfortable doing so. In Ephesians 4, Paul describes not only the scope of ministry responsibility, but also the necessity.

> It was he [Christ] who gave some to be apostles, some to be prophets, some to be evangelists, and some to be pastors and teachers, to prepare God's people for works of service, so that the body of Christ may be built up until we all reach unity in the faith and in the knowledge of the Son of God and become mature, attaining to the whole measure of the fullness of Christ. Then we will no longer be infants, tossed back and forth by the waves, and blown here and there by every wind of teaching and by the cunning and craftiness of men in their deceitful scheming. Instead, speaking the truth in love, we will in all things grow up into him who is the Head, that is, Christ. From him the whole body, joined and held together by every supporting ligament, grows and builds itself up in love, as each part does its work.
> Ephesians 4:11-16

Note the division of labor. There are two groups of people in the church: those who equip and those who need to be equipped for works of service. The word translated *service* is the common Greek term for *ministry*. Also note that the two groups are not the leaders and the followers, the ministers and the pew sitters, or the performers and the spectators. Everyone's job is *ministry*, and *everyone* has a significant contribution to make.

According to this passage, when we all step up to serve— female *and* male—good things happen. The church grows, spiritually and numerically. The immature become more mature. The naive become more discerning. The unstable become more anchored. The un-Christlike become more Christlike. The infirm become more healthy.

But what happens when men choose to sit passively on the sidelines? The church doesn't grow. The immature become stunted. The naive are deceived. The unstable are shipwrecked. The entire body becomes sickly. Without a doubt, when we fail to lead and take our faith seriously, the consequences are costly. George Gallup says: "Women may be the backbone of the congregation, but the presence of a significant number of men is often a clear indicator of spiritual health."

What matters in the church is not religion but the form of Christ, and its taking form amidst a band of men.
DIETRICH BONHOEFFER

Our lack of spiritual involvement as men impacts a lot of other individuals besides us. As men have bailed, so have young people. The church is hemorrhaging youth faster today than any preceding generation. Might it be because men are not setting the pace and spiritual fathers are rare? We've already discovered that spiritually passive fathers can stunt their children's faith. The same may very likely be true when "spiritual fathers" are lacking in a congregation! Even women are dropping out of church these days: Barna research reports the church attendance among women declined 20 percent in the 1990s.[6]

Perhaps those outside the church are hurt the worst. Because of how they're wired, females naturally focus on people within the church—making the "family" safe and secure. Nurturing one another becomes a higher priority than reaching out to non-Christians, some of whom are unsavory and perceived as a threat to the safety of the body. While we were discussing the unfriendliness of a certain church, a colleague of mine told me that the matriarchs of that church worked hard to keep the "gene pool" up to their standards. Maybe that's why for every eighty-five people who attend church, only one person comes to Christ in a given year.[7] It seems that no one benefits from the disappearance of men from church.

2. Grasp the manly side of ministry. It would be easy to assume that Ephesians 4 is all about warm relationships—and certainly that is a strong component. Protecting and nurturing are important and needed ministries, but they tend to be the more feminine values of ministry and only part of what is needed. But there is a more masculine component as well.

Ministry is not all soft and sentimental. There is something to build, grow, and establish within the body of Christ where a man can get his hands dirty. More than that, the purpose of the church is not to make each other feel good. There is a serious goal—the highest ambition—toward which to strive, reach for, and exert ourselves. There is nothing comfortable about it. And don't miss this: It is a risky adventure. There is a treacherous sea to cross. In the war between God's Kingdom and Satan's, there are enemies to fight, threats to brave, and "fifth column" elements to confront. Sure, love and unity are important, but so is speaking the truth frankly and candidly to ourselves and our comrades in arms. And yes, there are also wounds to nurse. But the church is not a hospital. It is an army taking back enemy-held territory that happens to have a M.A.S.H. unit to restore the wounded so they can get back in the battle, not to hold their hands and make them feel better about themselves. There is a great work to be done, and it requires us all, a strong band of brothers (along with our sisters), doing our very best to achieve God's goal.

Church is not for sissies and neither was Jesus. He was gentle, but He also made things with His bare hands. He was kind, but He commanded the loyalty of coarse fishermen, called out powerful preachers, whipped dishonest merchants, and stood toe-to-toe with unjust judges. He was tender and loving, but being "nice" doesn't get a man crucified. Dorothy Sayers (gotta love this woman) wrote, "We have very efficiently pared the claws of the Lion of Judah, certified Him 'meek and mild,' and recommended Him as a fitting household pet for pale curates and pious old ladies."[8]

Are you being led to worship a "domesticated" Jesus on Sunday morning? Is He a kinder, gentler version of the person we see in the Gospels made over by His current, self-appointed PR agents? Have hymns and songs that speak of war and struggle and victory and defeat been replaced by sweet tunes and romantic songs about Him? If so, stand up and lead. Don't be obnoxious about it. You may need to help ministry leaders see the need to live out the manly side of Jesus. If they fail to get what you're talking about, don't be an emotional lightweight and pitch a fit. Take responsibility for yourself and your own worship. While everyone else is singing romantic choruses to Jesus, pause and thank Him for His love along with everyone else, but don't stop there. Let your mind go to the power and might that Jesus exerted in the fight to save you from the enemy.

Don't expect applause when you bring up this idea of the masculine side of Jesus. Some women may question your motives and your maturity. Claws may even come out. And some men—who've grown accustomed to passivity—may resist your push to get them off the sidelines and into the game.

However, the risk will be worth it because other men will be stirred by the longing to be the man God created us all to be. Once you find these men, stick tight. You need each other.

3. **Don't let the church squeeze you into its mold.** In chapter 6 you saw how easy it is to follow someone else's agenda for your life rather than God's. As you begin to gain a firmer grasp on who God created you to be—and who He didn't create you to be—you'll be less likely to be conformed to other people's expectations. Don't be tempted to abandon your desire to serve in ways most compatible with your gifts simply because of your church's need for long-term volunteers in other areas.

In some churches, even those men who choose to accept a leadership position may be in for a rude surprise. They may be criticized if they are bold or decisive. On a number of occasions I've seen this crush the enthusiasm and drive of a high-octane leader who accepted a position on a church board. These men were not egotistical, domineering males who had to have things their way, but powerful leaders who wanted to serve. When feminine values dominate church life, decisions often are made at the speed of a garden slug because everyone must be sensitive to everyone else's *feelings*. Issues are talked to death, and simple decisions can take months. Don't misunderstand me. These aspects are important, but not at the expense of prolonging a decision past the point of it needing to be made because someone or some group's feelings may be hurt.

> *The most useful members of a church are usually those who would be doing harm if they were not doing good.*
> CHARLES SPURGEON

Here's an example of what I mean. When Greg learned about the plight of hundreds of refugees who lived within walking distance of his church, he was deeply concerned. He "adopted" a family to help through one of the international refugee agencies, but when Greg began working with his family, he recognized a huge problem. There were plenty of resources available—health care, child care, transportation, job training—but these resources were not easily accessible either to the refugees or to their sponsoring families.

Greg proposed, and even offered to fund, the creation of a Web site where people looking for help could find links to the resources they needed to help their refugee families. When Greg came to his church with this idea and a passion to get others involved, he was immediately asked to join the community outreach committee. For months they had been studying the needs of the refugee community and discussing what the church could do. They needed leadership to make a decision about what actions to take, but after three meetings, Greg was fit to be tied. He felt as if he had wasted three evenings meeting with a group that would rather talk about a problem than do something about it—and he wanted to do something! He graciously sidestepped the committee and made his idea for a Web site happen on his own. Now rather than spending hours on the phone trying to connect with the right person at the right agency, refugees and their sponsors can go to one spot to find the information they need.

All this to say: be careful. A church can have a mold of its own just like the world does, and it can be just as deadly to you as a man. Don't let anything or anyone squeeze you into something you are not. Saying yes to someone else's agenda, no matter how worthy or spiritual it might sound, can lead you to say *no* to the thing God wants you to do.

Nonetheless, you are still responsible to give yourself away to other Christians. As you do, you may be surprised to turn around and find that a number of people follow when you take the initiative to lead yourself.

Living as a Faithful Steward

In chapter after chapter, you've read about responsibility—and responsibility always means risk. Any time we take responsibility, we put our manhood on the line—sometimes even in the church.

In chapter 4 we saw that to become the leader God calls us to be we must first follow Jesus, the ultimate leader. That means we must stop trying to protect the identity we've created for ourselves and instead find our true identity in Christ. It's only when we deny and crucify the résumé and reputation we craft about ourselves and become reckless with our status that we can truly serve others. And it's only when we know that we get our name from God that we have the courage to lead with reckless abandon. G. K. Chesterton, British writer of the early twentieth century, gave a good description of this abandonment and what it takes.

> Courage is almost a contradiction in terms. It means a strong desire to live taking the form of a readiness to die. "He that will lose his life, the same shall save it," is not a piece of mysticism for saints and heroes. It is a piece of everyday advice for sailors or mountaineers. It might be printed in an Alpine guide or a drill book. The paradox is the whole principle of courage.

A man cut off by the sea may save his life if he will risk it on the precipice. He can only get away from death by continually stepping within an inch of it. A soldier surrounded by enemies, if he is to cut his way out, needs to combine a strong desire for living with a strange carelessness about dying. He must not merely cling to life, for then he will be a coward, and will not escape. He must not merely wait for death, for then that would be suicide, and he will not escape. He must seek his life in a spirit of furious indifference to it.[9]

1. Do you feel comfortable at church? What characteristics of your church attract men? What might repel them?

2. Contrast your level of comfort at a ball game and at church.

3. Can you point to men in your church who model what a serious commitment to Christ as a man looks like? What makes them stand out as men and as Christ followers?

4. What gifts has God given you that your church needs?

5. As you consider Chesterton's words above in light of your involvement at church, do you see any way in which you need to courageously step into responsibility?

6. Has God placed a dream on your heart that could best be worked out through the church?

7. How might you encourage those within your church to welcome non-Christians into your body? to work to influence culture rather than attempt to barricade the church doors against it?

Since, then, you have been raised with Christ, set your hearts on things above, where Christ is seated at the right hand of God. Set your minds on things above, not on earthly things. For you died, and your life is now hidden with Christ in God.
COLOSSIANS 3:1-3

Leadership, according to the One who put the principle into practice in the first place, is not the "rarest and most precious" of human capital, as an author put it. It's the common response of faithful men who recognize they have a responsibility to act without waiting to be told what to do. Leadership is rare today because it's always easier to shirk our duty and depend on other people to do the thinking and acting for us. However, the easiest or most cowardly response is often the most dangerous and difficult in the long run. As men, our most difficult task is to recognize that indeed we are not our own.

We've looked at a lot of areas of responsibilities in this book, but they all come back to the same point: The God who created and redeemed us has made us His steward-leaders over His creation. Our identity and destiny are not in our own hands, but in our Master's. C. S. Lewis puts it this way:

The terrible thing, the almost impossible thing, is to hand over your whole self—all your wishes and precautions—to Christ. But it is far easier than what we are trying to do instead. For what we are trying to do is to remain what we call "ourselves," to keep personal happiness as our great aim in life, and yet at the same time be "good." We are trying to let our mind and heart go their own way—centered on money or pleasure or ambition—and hoping, in spite of this, to behave honestly and chastely and humbly. And that is exactly what Christ warned us you could not do.[1]

But how do you go about this hard work of putting yourself in God's hands so you can be the leader He wants you to be? Lewis suggests that you "pretend" that you are indeed what God calls you to be. In the following I draw unashamed from Lewis's thoughts, for he has greatly influenced my thinking on the topic. Lewis suggests that often the only way to acquire a Christlike quality is to begin behaving as if you already have that attribute—which, as a new creation in Christ, you already do.[2]

As you begin to act on a daily basis as if something God says about you is true, the way you look at yourself begins to change. As this happens, you will begin to recognize that some of the things you think and do don't fit with your new identity in Christ. You may see that, as Lewis says, "instead of saying your prayers, you ought to be downstairs ... helping your wife wash up" because you realize as a good steward-leader that's what you should be doing right then.

What's happening is that at the moment you choose to follow Christ, believe what He has made you to be, and do the thing you know you ought to do, He is changing your pretense into reality. This is not simply a reprogramming of your mind, however. It is an inside-out renewal that brings a transforming effect on your life, choice by choice, day by day. This is exactly what Paul describes in Romans 12.

> *Therefore, I urge you, brothers, in view of God's mercy, to offer your bodies as living sacrifices, holy and pleasing to God— this is your spiritual act of worship. Do not conform any longer to the pattern of this world, but be transformed by the renewing of your mind. Then you will be able to test and approve what God's will is—his good, pleasing and perfect will.* Romans 12:1-2

The wonderful thing is that this really isn't pretend. It is reality. You have become a new creation in Christ, and He is walking with you every step of the way. Just as He walked with Adam in the cool of the Garden, He walks with you in the heat of your daily challenges. Lewis describes the process like this.

> The real Son of God is at your side. He is beginning to turn you into the same kind of thing as Himself. He is beginning so to speak, to "inject" His kind of life and thought, His *Zoe*, into you; beginning to turn a tin soldier into a live man. The part that does not like it is the part that is still tin.[3]

The path of a leader is an uphill climb, and you simply can't make the journey without the greatest servant-leader Himself. Don't wait for someone else to lead. While in one way it is the hard path, in another it is far easier than trying to control your own destiny, which always keeps you on a road that leads to destruction. Commit yourself to Jesus and follow Him into the service to which He calls you. And may you be found faithful. My prayer for us all is that when we stand before our Master, we will each hear these beautiful words from Matthew 25:21:

Living the good life is frequently dull, flat, and commonplace. Our greatest need is to make life fiery, creative, and capable of spiritual struggle.
NIKOLAI BERDYAEV

> Well done, good and faithful servant! You have been faithful with a few things; I will put you in charge of many things. Come and share your master's happiness!

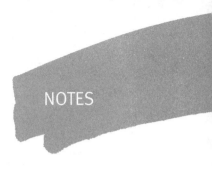

NOTES

Introduction

1. David Gergen, "America's Best Leaders," posted 10/22/06, http://www.usnews
.com/usnews/news/articles/061022/30opener.htm; accessed 4/13/07. This story
appears in the October 30, 2006, print edition of *U.S. News and World Report*.
2. Ibid.
3. Larry Crabb, *The Silence of Adam* (Grand Rapids: Zondervan, 1995), 12.
4. For a few biblical instructions on leadership, see Jeremiah 29:7; Ephesians
4:15-16; Colossians 3:19, 21; 4:5-6; and 1 Timothy 2:8; 3:4.

Chapter 1: Wanted: A New Kind of Leader

1. Bill George, "Truly Authentic Leadership," posted 9/22/06; http://www.usnews
.com/usnews/news/articles/061022/30authentic_2.htm; accessed 4/13/07.
This story appears in the October 30, 2006, print edition of *U.S. News and
World Report*.
2. Exodus 12:37 tells us that there were 600,000 adult males in the Exodus, about
the size of Napoleon's Russian invasion army. This number does not include
women and children, however. Scholars estimate the number of people in the
Exodus between two and three million.
3. A study conducted by the Center for Creative Leadership found that 85
percent of respondents believed the definition of effective leadership has
changed in the last five years. André Martin, "The Changing Nature of
Leadership," (Center for Creative Leadership, 2006); available at http://www.
ccl.org/leadership/research/projects.aspx.

Chapter 2: Everyday Leaders

1. Peter Block, *Stewardship: Choosing Service Over Self-Interest* (San Francisco:
Berrett-Koehler Publishers, 1993), xx.
2. C. S. Lewis, *Mere Christianity* (New York: Simon and Schuster, 1996),
126–127.
3. Michael Novak, *Business as a Calling* (New York: Simon and Schuster, 1996),
18, 38.

Chapter 3: The Leaders God Intended

1. Sonny and Cher, "I Got You Babe," from their album *Look At Us* (Sundazed Music, Inc., 1965).
2. 1 Timothy 2:14

Chapter 4: Following the Real Leader

1. C. S. Lewis, *The Problem of Pain* (New York: HarperCollins, 2002), 91.
2. Tony Dungy, *Quiet Strength* (Carol Stream, IL: Tyndale House Publishers, 2007), 50–51.
3. Ibid., 291.
4. The Hebrew word for soul, *nephish*, is virtually parallel in meaning to *psyche*.

Chapter 5: Don't Miss Your Calling

1. John Pollock, *William Wilberforce: A Man Who Changed His Times* (Burke, VA: The Trinity Forum, 1996), 11.
2. Ibid., 13.
3. In today's terms, moral values.
4. Pollock, *William Wilberforce: A Man Who Changed His Times*, 11.
5. Nancy Pearcey, *Total Truth* (Wheaton, IL: Crossway Books, 2004), 48–49.

Chapter 6: Discovering Your Destiny

1. If you want to bring this kind of assessment to your church or experience this process guided by a professional, contact The Giftedness Center. Read about their services at http://www.thegiftednesscenter.com.
2. John Pollock, *William Wilberforce: A Man Who Changed His Times*, 11.

Chapter 7: Why Women Need Men (and Vice Versa)

1. Carol Ann Culbert Johnson, "Men, Who Needs Them?" *Ezine Articles*, January 18, 2006.
2. C. S. Lewis, *The Four Loves* (San Diego: Harcourt, 1988), 61, 66–67.

Chapter 8: Bringing Out a Woman's Beauty

1. Amy Gillentine, "The Price of Vanity," *The Colorado Springs Business Journal*, August 31, 2007 http://www.csbj.com/story.cfm?ID=11016 (accessed November 7, 2007); Christine Bittar, "NPD: Prestige Color Cosmetics Beat Fragrance, Skincare Products," *Marketing Daily*, April 19, 2007, http://publications.mediapost.com/index.cfm?fuseaction=Articles.showArticle&art_aid=58955 (accessed November 7, 2007).
2. C. S. Lewis, *Mere Christianity* (New York: Simon and Schuster, 1996), 115.
3. Ibid., 116.

Chapter 9: The Wind beneath Her Wings

1. You can learn more at www.familymanager.com.
2. Available on the Free page at http://www.familymanager.com.

Chapter 10: The Inestimable Value of a Father

1. Barna Update, "Virginia Tech Tragedy is a Wake-Up Call to Parents," April 23,

2007; http://www.barna.org/FlexPage.aspx?Page=BarnaUpdateNarrowPreview&BarnaUpdateID=269.

2. Ibid.

3. Ibid.

4. David Blankenhorn, *Fatherless America* (New York: BasicBooks, 1995), 1–2.

5. "Survey on Child Health," U.S. Department of Health and Human Services, National Center for Health Statistics (Washington, DC: GPO, 1993).

6. Ibid.

7. Karen Heimer, "Gender, Interaction, and Delinquency: Testing a Theory of Differential Social Control," *Social Psychology Quarterly* 59 (1996): 39–61.

8. John O. G. Billy, Karin L. Brewster, and William R. Grady, "Contextual Effects on the Sexual Behavior of Adolescent Women," *Journal of Marriage and Family* 56 (1994): 381–404.

9. E. M. Krampe and P. D. Fairweather, "Father Presence and Family Formation: A Theoretical Reformulation," *Journal of Family Issues* 14, no. 4 (December 1993): 572–591.

10. "Fathers' Involvement in Their Children's Schools" National Center for Education Statistics (Washington DC: GPO, 1997).

11. Richard Koestner, Carol Franz, and Joel Weinberger, "The Family Origins of Empathic Concern: A Twenty-Six Year Longitudinal study," *Journal of Personality and Social Psychology* 58 (1990): 709–717.

12. George Alan Rekers, "Psychological Foundations for Rearing Masculine Boys and Feminine Girls," *Recovering Biblical Manhood and Womanhood: A Response to Evangelical Feminism*, Wayne Grudem and John Piper, eds. http://www.leaderu.com/orgs/cbmw/rbmw/chapter17.html (accessed 4/10/07).

13. Ibid.

14. Barna Research Online, "Women Are the Backbone of Christian Congregations in America," 6 March 2000, www.barna.org.

15. Bob Horner, Ron Ralston, and David Sunde, *Promise Keepers at Work* (Colorado Springs: Focus on the Family, 1996), 111.

16. Luke 19:9; Acts 10:2, 11:13-14; Acts 16:31-33; Acts 18:8; 1 Corinthians 1:16.

Chapter 11: Launching Children into the World

1. Courtney Lee, "Meet Zach Hunter—The Teenage Abolitionist," *Christianity Today*, posted Thursday, February 22, 2007. http://www.christiantoday.com/article/meet.zach.hunter.the.teenage.abolitionist/9640.htm.

2. "Just 15, He Leads Fight to Abolish Slavery" ABC News, *Good Morning America*, http://abcnews.go.com/GMA/story?id=2951434&page=1

3. Zach Hunter, *Be the Change: Your Guide to Freeing Slaves and Changing the World* (Grand Rapids, MI: Zondervan, 2007), 13.

Chapter 12: Your Monday Morning Mission

1. Check out America's Family at http://www.amfol.com and Steve's book at www.theboxyougot.com. You'll see why Steve is a Kingdom hero and why many former employees come back to talk with him about Jesus.

2. Dorothy Sayers, *Creed or Chaos?* (Manchester, NH: Sophia Institute Press, 1995), 77.

3. C. S. Lewis, *The Weight of Glory* (New York: Macmillan Publishing Company, 1980), 13.

Chapter 13: Stewards of the Message

1. Rodney Stark, *The Rise of Christianity: A Sociologist Reconsiders History* (Princeton, NJ: Princeton University Press, 1996), 6.

2. George Barna, *Evangelism that Works* (Ventura, CA: Regal Books, 1995), 22.

3. To learn more about faith flags and other ways to casually share your faith in the workplace, see *Going Public with Your Faith* by William Carr Peel and Walt Larimore (Grand Rapids: Zondervan, 2004).

4. John Pollock, *William Wilberforce: A Man Who Changed His Times*, 18.

Chapter 14: A Leader's Place in the World

1. George Barna, *The Second Coming of the Church* (Nashville: Word Publishing, 1998).

2. Kary Oberbrunner, *The Journey Towards Relevance* (Orlando, FL: Relevant Books, 2004), 46–47.

3. Timothy George, "Theology for an Age of Terror," *Christianity Today*, September 2006, vol. 50, no. 9, http://www.christianitytoday.com/ct/2006/september/1.78.html.

4. Ibid.

5. In this section I have drawn from Dr. Timothy J. Keller's thoughts on cultural impact, particularly from a message entitled "The Meaning of the City," October 5, 2003. It is available for purchase online in Redeemer's online sermon store at http://sermons.redeemer.com/store/index.cfm?fuseaction= product.display&Product_ID=18157&CFID=1294112&CFTOKEN= 31310346.

6. Rodney Stark, *The Rise of Christianity* (New York: HarperCollins, 1997), 82.

7. Ibid., 93.

Chapter 15: Stepping Out of the Pew

1. Barna Research Online, "Women Are the Backbone of Christian Congregations in America," 6 March 2000, www.barna.org.

2. Ibid.

3. Leon J. Podles, *The Church Impotent: The Feminization of Christianity* (Dallas: Spence Publishing, 1999), ix.

4. David Murrow, *Why Men Hate Going to Church* (Nashville: Nelson Books, 2005), 4–5.

5. Ibid, 51.

6. Barna Research Online, "Women Are the Backbone of Christian Congregations."

7. Thom S. Rainer, *Surprising Insights from the Unchurched and Proven Ways to Reach Them* (Grand Rapids, MI: Zondervan, 2001), 36.

NOTES

8. Dorothy L. Sayers, *Creed or Chaos?* 6.

9. G. K. Chesterton, *Collected Works* (San Francisco: Ignatius Press, 1986), 277.

Conclusion

1. C. S. Lewis, *Mere Christianity* (New York: Simon & Schuster, 1996), 170.

2. Ibid., 162–167.

3. Ibid., 164.

FREE BONUS CHAPTER
BY BILL PEEL
AVAILABLE AT
www.christianbookguides.com

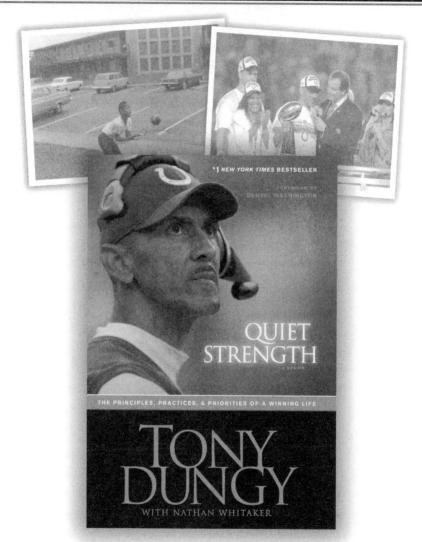